How Ex

25 Surefire Recipes for Sabotaging Your Career

Lee Thayer

Author of
Leadership: Thinking, Being, Doing

WME Books
a division of
Windsor Media Enterprises, LLC
Rochester, New York
USA

How Executives Fail:
25 Surefire Recipes for Sabotaging Your Career

ISBN-10: 1-934229-00-8
ISBN-13: 978-1-934229-00-2

Editor: Yvonne DiVita
Cover Design: Karin Marlett Choi
Page Layout/Design: Tom Collins

Published by:
WME Books
Windsor Media Enterprises, LLC
Rochester, New York
USA

Available online at: www.WMEBooks.com, as well as other booksellers and distributors worldwide.

Special Sales:

This and other WME Books titles are available at special discounts for bulk purchases, for use in sales promotions, or as premiums. Special editions, including personalized covers, excerpts of existing books, and corporate imprints, can be created in large quantities for special needs or projects.

For more information, please contact:

Special Book Orders
Windsor Media Enterprises, LLC
282 Ballad Avenue
Rochester, NY 14626

1-877-947-BOOK (2665)

info@wmebooks.com

Praise for *How Executives Fail*:

"Habit is a great deadener and this book will help you break the ones that could fatally end your career (and ambitions!). The best 'insurance' book on leadership I've read."

– **Warren Bennis**,
Distinguished Professor of Business,
University of Southern California,
Author of ***On Becoming a Leader***

"Every few centuries, in every field of study, someone arises whose insights dwarf those of his or her peers. Lee Thayer is one of them. His work and his name will be remembered for centuries to come. As Einstein eclipsed Newton, Thayer eclipses Machiavelli. His seminal thinking on leadership is the foundation for all that I have done at Johnsonville Sausage."

– **Ralph C. Stayer**, CEO
Johnsonville Sausage

"With characteristic insight, Lee Thayer tells us there are two ways to succeed: 'get lucky and avoid failure.' (Absolutely brilliant!) Since you can't learn luck, Thayer offers his readers a baker's two dozen ways to 'fail on purpose' in this original, funny, and useful little gem of a book. Smart executives will sneak peeks at its ***ironically*** practical pages when no one is looking."

– **James O'Toole**, author of
Creating the Good Life

"In my work with top executives, I have come into contact with the many hundreds of books about leadership published in the last 30 years – and with the many hundreds of executives who look to that outpouring for some reliable ways of improving their skills and their organizations. From that view, Lee Thayer's book, ***Leadership: Thinking, Being, Doing***, is the best damn book on leadership there is. Now, in his inimitable way, he has turned the "how-to-succeed" literature on its head. Behind the humor and irony of ***How Executives Fail***, you will uncover the most provocative and practical voice in leadership today. Thayer teases us solidly onto the path of superior and sustainable performance by revealing how most executives fail. What a coup!"

– **Pat Murray**, President
J. P. Murray and Associates

More praise for ***How Executives Fail***:

"Attracted by his (often) counter-intuitive but extremely practical ideas, I invited Lee Thayer a few years ago to be my on-demand coach and mentor. The fabulous successes we have been experiencing at Phillips Corporation are in large measure a result of his guidance. His unique perspectives in ***Leadership: Thinking, Being, Doing*** have been our compass. In his newest and most provocative book, ***How Leaders Fail: 25 Surefire Recipes for Sabotaging Your Career***, he turns conventional wisdoms on their head. My advice? Don't even think about attempting high-performance leadership without first studying the writings of the master."

– **Alan M. Phillips**, President,
Phillips Corporation

"Once again Lee Thayer has challenged CEOs to step up and think outside the box. The supreme master of counter-intuition, he beckons leaders to confront themselves. Thayer is high-performance leadership's modern day Yoda. No other book is needed (and I surveyed – ugh! – 5,000 or so of the best of them) to understand leadership competency and organizational effectiveness than Thayer's earlier book, ***Leadership: Thinking, Being, Doing***. Now comes Dr. Thayer's latest gift to CEOs and key executives: ***How Executives Fail: 25 Surefire Recipes for Sabotaging Your Career***. There is no set of ideas on leadership more profound, no executive competency more revealed, no recipes for results more useful than Lee Thayer's latest illumination of what really counts for leaders who want to make a dent in the Universe."

– **Michael W. Norris**,
Senior Chairman,
Vistage (The World's Largest CEO Membership Organization)

"When I assumed the role of CEO at HarrisInteractive a couple of years ago, I knew I wanted to do everything in my power to make a "great" organization, an organization that benefits all of its stakeholders. This is what Lee Thayer refers to in his popular book, ***Leadership: Thinking, Being, Doing***, as a "high-performance" organization. With our level of commitment, we enticed him on board to help us in our quest, bringing to bear his decades of experience. We now have ten initiatives underway that seem to be making a profound difference in attitudes and performance throughout the organization. In his new book, ***How Executives Fail***, he provides executives with some cautionary tales – including the tongue-in-cheek advice that a necessary condition of success is not to fail. His ironic twist lends itself to humor, while being deadly serious. His is a remarkably unique voice in an otherwise overcrowded space. He knows what he is talking about, and he knows how to do it. If you want to know how to make a great organization, consult the ranking coach."

– **Gregory T. Novak**,
Harris Interactive, Inc.

"As an ex-CEO, I am now devoted to helping CEOs achieve a better life, at work and at home. There is no comparable resource, in my opinion, than Lee Thayer – whether in his writings (e.g., ***Leadership: Thinking, Being, Doing***) or in front of the participants in our seminars and workshops. He understands high-performance organizations, and the leader's role in making it happen in a more practical way than anyone else. Our members love him. His latest, ***How Executives Fail***, is a stunning achievement – full of intrigue, innuendo, good humor and just plain inescapable facts about executive life. You'll want a copy for everyone on your staff, and for your peers."

– **Bruce W. Peters**,
Founder of CEOHQ Fellows
and Co-Founder of PeerHQ

It takes some people all their lives
to become failures, while others
achieve it in just a few years.

– American folklore

Irony: *"a state of affairs or an event*
that seems deliberately contrary
to what one expects
and is often amusing as a result."

– The New Oxford American Dictionary

"How many people are trapped
in their everyday habits:
part numb, part frightened, part indifferent?
To have a better life we must
keep choosing how we're living."

– Albert Einstein

Overview

For all those who would presume to manage a human enterprise, there are two ways of succeeding: One is to get lucky. The other is to avoid failing.

It may seem perverse, but there are also two ways of failing:

One is to follow one's peers lemming-like down the slippery slope of mediocrity.

The other is to be oblivious to what part of the problem you are.

> Two ways to fail:
>
> Follow the mediocre
>
> or
>
> Remain oblivious

What is *common* to all situations is not the likelihood of success, but the likelihood of failure. The everyday rate of any real success on the part of managers and executives seems to bear no correlation to the exponential flood of advice about "how to succeed."

This little book of recipes about how to fail as a manager or executive turns that flood of advice about how to succeed on its head. The indispensable factor is not a list of explanations about how somebody succeeded. The indispensable factor is simply that of avoiding failure – avoiding the kind of thinking and actions that make failure likely.

There isn't a manager alive who couldn't use this book to advantage.

Hardly anyone sets out to fail. But most managers and executives do fail. They fail their own hopes and aspirations, if not their roles. How do they *do* this? By the time they figure out by trial and error what part of the problem they are, it's usually too late.

This little book is the only instruction book you'll ever need about how to avoid failing by default. You'll learn how to fail on purpose, with dash and aplomb. You'll meet many familiar people - people you will immediately recognize – in these pages. Here and there, you might catch a glimpse of yourself.

Think of it as failure therapy. What you can't learn here about your personal talents for failing you'll just have to learn the hard away. By doing so. If you don't have insight into how executives fail, you're likely to end up where you don't want to go.

Enjoy this small book of collected wisdom about how to fail. Each "recipe" is drawn from universals of real life – how most managers and executives have failed in spite of their best intentions.

Annotated Recipe List

[This book is not composed of chapters that continue on from the previous. It consists of short pieces – 5 to 8 pages – that I call "recipes." These can be read one at a time profitably – by choice or by happenstance. These annotated titles will provide the reader with all the clues needed to get into and gain from the book, and are largely self-explanatory.]

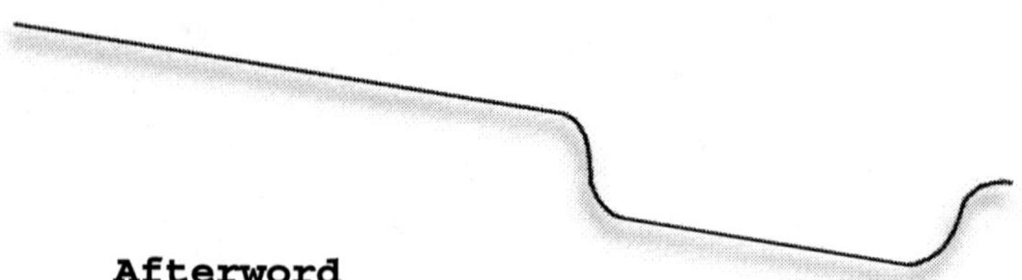

25 Recipes

By Way of An Introduction

"How can we fail
when we're so sincere?"

– Charlie Brown

Just so you will know ... I have walked in the shoes of those executives and wannabes who may find the ironic stance of this book not only entertaining but useful. In addition to functioning as an executive/CEO (more or less successfully), I've worked and consulted with people in that role for just under five decades. I have conducted seminars for many, many hundreds of them on this planet.

I have been a trusted consultant to a wide range of executives in every industry and of every size. And I have partnered with them as a coach in developing their leadership in order to make truly high-performance organizations. They are therefore my friends, my peers, my fellow travelers.

I do not malign them by taking the position that most CEOs will *fail.* Most *will* fail – minimally, their own expectations, if nothing else. They will fall short of their own hopes and dreams.

At the end, they will not be ecstatic about their lives on earth. Many will live in frustration and they will die in frustration, because they will not have achieved what they envisioned when they were young, or when they first took over their role as executive or CEO. They may exhibit outward bravado. They may take on all of the trappings of success by accumulating the stuff that signals success in our society – wealth, material things, and a way of walking and talking as if superior to those who have accumulated less.

Now, what does it mean to be holding a book of recipes about "how-to" *fail*?

Consider the following:

- More than 10,000 books about how to succeed as a manager or an executive have been published in the past couple of decades. And this doesn't count the many more thousands of seminars on how to succeed. All this effort and all this expenditure does not seem to have changed the rate of failure.

  So the perverse logic is this: If you can study how to succeed and still manage to fail, maybe you could study how managers and executives have failed and thereby get some clues about how at least to avoid failing in the ways they did.

- There are few books at Amazon.com about how to fail. This, in spite of the fact that most managers and executives do fail. *Where are they learning how to do this?* Up to now, they've had to learn it on the street.

With *How Executives Fail* you can look into their executive offices, and learn for yourself how they failed. In order that you may – masterfully – fail, if you so wish. With intent and aplomb. Or, perhaps you can appreciate the irony of coming at it this way. And thus learn not so much how to succeed, but how to avoid failing. At least how to avoid failing in the ways so many of your predecessors and your contemporaries have. Or will.

- We all know that others will not consider an executive especially sane if he or she sets out to fail. Still, most will fail. *Mediocrity* is not the same as excelling. Maybe it's only a mild form of failure. Some have failed spectacularly, as the business press tells us. But most just sort of fizzled out along the way. We don't hear much about them. Where or what is the black hole that sucked them into mediocrity against their will and their intentions?

- Here's a puzzling fact. Executives who fail are *more likely* to be avid consumers of the flood of literature on "how to succeed" than are those few who actually do succeed. So, is it not ironic that they may be getting plenty of advice from the business press about how to *fail*? All that "how to succeed" advice is cleverly packaged to seduce the unwary into thinking they could succeed if only they bought the next great book or the next seminar promoting the latest or most popular panacea. Billions are spent every year on executive education. Days and weeks are lost, while executives "train" to be better than they are. But all of our problems have not gone away, have they?

- Here is what's truly ironic. People seem to be infinitely creative about how to fail. Maybe they didn't pick it up from a guru. But keep in mind that the sale of his or her next book depends not upon the success of the readers, but *on their failures*. After all, if the book succeeded, and the readers succeeded, these gurus would be out of a job, wouldn't they?

- Finally, it's plain wrong for thousands of managers and executives to spend many billions to collect the currently-fashionable ideas about how to succeed when most of them are going to fail anyway. Doesn't it make sense to make use of the principles that have contributed to their failure – to reveal the secrets of how they failed?

None of these people, on whom so much of our future depends, *wants* to fail. Or in the case of this book, wants to learn how to fail. So my theme in this book is not really how to "fail." My expectation, rather, is that by taking this tongue-in-cheek approach, by assuming a posture of irony, a great many useful ideas about how to actually *avoid* failing might emerge.

Not one of the leaders I have worked with has, to my knowledge, aimed for mediocrity. And yet many ended up there. The fall into mediocrity is surely not to be counted as any form of success. And since being mediocre was not their aim in life, it seems fair to assume that, in that sense, they have failed – because they did not fulfill their own purposes, their own hopes and dreams, in life. Many of those who failed, or will fail, do so as a result of contributing unintentionally to their own failure, either because of their own personal dragons (following bad advice, making bad choices/decisions), or simply as a result of their personal but ultimately wrongheaded ways of thinking and of doing things.

After decades of direct in-the-trenches experience, that's what I concluded. Maybe those few who have succeeded were just plain lucky. And maybe the bulk of those who have failed were just plain unlucky. But check out the logic here. If there is an ever-growing flood of books, lectures, seminars, etc., purporting to tell you how to succeed without being lucky, then maybe there should be this one book that provides you with tried-and-true recipes for how to fail without bumbling along waiting for Lady Luck to deal you a lousy hand.

This book reveals many secrets about how to fail. If you want to be a celebrity failure, this book tells you how to do it, purposefully and with flair. You won't have to struggle and waste time learning via the grapevine how to fail, or by imitating a role model. Here are the key insider tips and secrets you need to fail strategically, rather than embarrassingly, by default. If you want to know how so many of your peers contributed to their own failure in their role as an executive, read on. If you want to expose yourself to an *ironic* but still very *serious* twist on how you might actually achieve more of your hopes and dreams as an executive, read on for sure.

25 Recipes for becoming a **celebrity** failure.

If you are looking for the pitfalls that make failures (or, perhaps, mediocrities) out of otherwise smart and ambitious people, then this book is for you. I have revealed the common denominators of how the majority of managers and executives succeed in failing. Maybe, cleverly, you could make use of the revelations offered … and avoid the failure train so many of your colleagues and peers are on.

One last note: The sequence of each of these little recipes for how to fail is not important. You could open the book at any page and find something useful to you, since failure, like success, is such an individual thing. And, since it probably takes as much luck to fail as it does to succeed, I wish you "Good Luck" in finding yourself – or your future – in these pages. So put your thinking cap on backwards and put a twinkle in your eye. Take a bite here and there, but always with that frame of mind that enables you to make the most of it for your purposes.

At the very least, enjoy this perverse approach!

Lee Thayer
Flat Rock, NC, USA
December 20, 2006

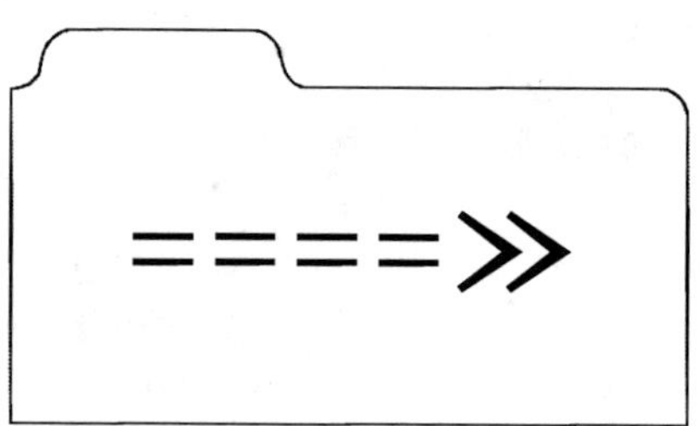

Recipe #1

How to Breed Failure from Success

Most managers and executives who fail … do so without really trying. If you are going to outdo them, you've got to try. You've got to think – really THINK – about the lessons to be learned, and practice them daily.

We're talking about intention here: focused, deliberate, and strategic. So, if you intend to fail on purpose – which is the only way you can take credit for it – here are a couple of basic lessons.

First lesson: If you understand – really understand – how even a small success in your life, if taken as a formula for your success today or tomorrow, can actually lead to your eventual failure, you can be more intentional about failing.

First Lesson:
Success, turned into a formula or theory for future success, leads to failure.

Think about it. Most people who experience some small success at anything will concoct a kind of "theory" about how they did it and then they'll apply that "theory" again and again. When it begins not to work, they'll blame the world. You can almost hear them thinking, "… can't be me. I was successful before by doing things this way."

Do they change their "success paradigm" when the 'usual' way no longer works? Nope, they try to change the world around them. And when the world doesn't change to their satisfaction, they rail at it.

The lesson is this: Make up a creative explanation of how you happened to be successful, and stick to it. **If you want to fail, be persistent in creating and nurturing your own "success paradigm."** You'll get there, far ahead of others, and far more efficiently. That's one of the basic lessons to be derived from thousands of executive failures.

Children do this, and we're amused. They get furious with the sock if they can't get it on. Seasoned executives do this all the time. They get angry when the world doesn't work the way their own heads do. No one finds their antics very amusing.

Here's lesson two on how to breed failure from success: Most people like to pretend that any success that comes their way is due to them. But, if they don't succeed … well, they have a larder full of excuses and explanations.

```
Second Lesson:

   Success = my credit

Failure = others' blame
```

While they attribute any success to themselves, these same people attribute their failures to any explanation they can "sell" to others. This is kind of the crux of the matter if you think about it.

Let's say that when you were a youngster you were rough-housing with a friend and broke a lamp in the house. Your mother was likely upset about it. She would stand over you, finger pointing in your face and ask, "Roscoe, did you do this?" You were probably thinking, "I wonder what kind of convincing story I can tell her about how this happened, an explanation that makes me an innocent bystander?" What she'll buy, you will sell.

Adults get to be really good at this because they've had a lifetime of practice. Yet, if you got an "A" on your report card, you wouldn't blame this on your pal in class or on the teacher, would you? You'd take credit for it. Maybe neither one was your "fault," neither the lamp nor the "A", but over the years you come to see yourself as the sole cause of things that get others' approval, and innocent of any outcomes that might get their disapproval.

When you've got that down, you are ready to get "a job." Once you have a job, and you become really good at using your own theories of success, you'll likely get promoted. After all, we want our managers and executives to be omniscient – to make good things happen – and it's okay for them to take credit for all of it. At the same time, we want them to be able to explain away any bad things that happen as not their fault. Keep in mind that your superiors are better at this game than you are, so they'll blame you for their failures. Move up so you can do this too. That's a common practice that actually gets rewarded.

The better you are at this, the better you will fail. It may take some others years to fail, but you've decided to do so on purpose. So, why put it off?

There's a Catch 22 here, of course. After all, who would believe you if you credited yourself for failures, but credited others (or conditions like "the economy") for successes? That would be much closer to the truth of the matter, but who would believe you? That's not the way celebrity success stories are purveyed by the media. The most popular ones are the "overnight" successes – who gain fame and fortune just for being "talented"! You play it the way it's played, and thus become blind to how failure – and success – actually happen.

Given this way of thinking –

- Since you cannot readily imagine that you are part of the cause of your failure, you never learn anything about what part of the problem you may have been. As Alan Cooper put it in his book, *The Inmates Are Running the Asylum*, **"The unfortunate side effect of not understanding failure is the silent admission that success is not predictable – that luck and happenstance rule the … world."** [Emphasis mine.]
- And, since you are confident that you are invariably the main cause of your success, you never learn what you need to learn about the other factors that have always played a role in any successes you may have had.

It's a way of stupidifying yourself in order to facilitate your failure. It's very common. In the end, if you consciously practice it, you can fail on purpose, surpassing all those others who fail by default.

History has proven that your peers have a very poor understanding of success and failure. Everyone is doing the "right" thing until the lights actually go out. If you can't get down to reality, you will be equally victimized by both your successes and your failures, just as they are.

Here's a role model for failure:

> *Hal was a go-getter from the git-go. He came into the company eager to blow everyone else away. So he got promoted on the basis of his enthusiasm, as often happens. He had some reasonable successes early on. Thinking that this meant he was superior to others, and that he therefore had the key to success,*

he continued to apply his very own "success paradigm" in every new situation that emerged. It hadn't occurred to him that luck and other people had played major roles in his early successes. His success paradigm was the real truth, to Hal.

He became arrogantly out of touch. The more he tried to apply the "secrets" of success from his earlier days, the more he failed. Because he blamed everything and everyone else for his increasing failures, and because he could only see himself, alone, as the cause of his success, he continued to fail. This did not affect his job, of course. He was kept around by people who shared his mind-set. At age 54, he had already been "out to pasture" for a couple of years. He was still hanging out there, but no one paid him any heed. To the younger managers, he was a joke. To his superiors, a nuisance. To himself, a victim.

There's a moral in there. If you can't find it, being victimized by your own "success paradigm" is almost assured.

Here's a hint: People see the world in terms of their explanations of it, their explanations being, for them, reality. So, a little success goes a long way. Even a small success goes to one's head. We want to relive it, over and over again. We cling to it, like a child clings to her magical, comforting blanket. Try taking that ragged old blanket away from her and see what happens – the little angel will turn into a ferocious "devil"! That's the way failing executives cling to their "theories."

William James once wrote to H. G. Wells about "the moral flabbiness born of the exclusive worship of the bitch-goddess SUCCESS."

Could he have meant "mental flabbiness" as well? "Success" often does function like a "bitch-goddess." Have you noticed?

People cling to the "theory" of success as they've created it. And reject the possibility of any culpability for their failures. So they never really understand either one. That's how failure gets bred from success. Way to go! **You can make it work for you if you simply practice taking credit for any success you may have, but blame others or blame "circumstances" for your failures.**

Every "motivational" speaker or writer in the Western world can tell you how to make success out of failure. There's a multi-billion-dollar industry devoted to it. And why are these books and seminars a growth industry, even in bad times? Because they don't work. So the same people need to attend the next one, buy the next book, be "true believers" in the magic of "success." Something like "Success for Dummies." Or, as Evan Esar, writer and humorist, put it: "Nothing succeeds like success, and nothing fails like reading a book on how to attain it."

That's because writers of that *Secrets of Success* book sitting on everyone's desk this week, are writing about how to make *success out of failure*. Something he or she couldn't do in real life, so they decided to write a book about it (see #6, "How to Maintain Your Gullibility"). As in, "those who cannot do, teach."

Those books that contain hundreds of success paradigms which executives carry around like trusty six-shooters will eventually start shooting blanks. The executives will be going through the motions, but the motions will no longer fit the facts. The theory or paradigm will have warped to fit the executives' needs, not the realities of a changing world.

So cling to your success paradigm no matter what. Failure will eventually be the product. Guaranteed.

Let me share an old but useful story:

> *A drunk lost the keys to his car. A kindly passer-by asked him, "Where did you lose your keys?"*
>
> *"Over there," the drunk replied, pointing to a dark alley.*
>
> *"Then why are you looking for them over here?" the passer-by wondered.*
>
> *"Because," the drunk replied, "the light is better over here under the streetlight."*

The executive who is destined to fail wields his "success paradigm" like that streetlight. As if enchanted by the beam of light cast by a long-ago bit of success, he expects that tiny beam of light, always growing dimmer, to illuminate every situation he will face. He provides evidence of the old adage, "Nothing breeds failure like success."

Why? Because success brings complacency. And complacency brings failure.

That, friend, is how you, too, can breed failure out of success. Little by little, but with certainty, your success paradigm will breed every problem common to failing managers and executives – every problem but success.

W. C. Fields had some advice for failure:

> *"If at first you don't succeed, try, try again. Then quit. There's no use being a damn fool about it."*

It takes a long time for most people to realize they have failed. But it isn't "cool" to fail just like everyone else does. Let your own unique success paradigm do it for you – and, instead of being like most others – cut to the chase.

Failing on purpose is noble failure. Failing by default is the clod's way out.

Recipe #2

How to "Achieve" Mediocrity

The notion that mediocrity is "achieved" surely brought a smile, or a smirk, to your face. Most people do achieve mediocrity. Few **intended** to achieve it. Fewer still had a **strategy** for doing so. Therefore, the competition for failing in this way is fierce. As the old adage goes, "The pursuit of mediocrity is always successful." So you're up against almost certain success by others. And they won't even be trying.

Mediocrity seems to function in (modern) society a bit like gravity. It does its best work when you give it no heed. Very much a "going with the flow" kind of thing. It's all downstream. All you have to do is let go. Like earth's gravity, it will pull you in with no effort on your part.

If you want to escape that destination, you have to muster something like escape velocity. You have to overcome the fantastic forces of mediocrity that prevail in everyday life, in order merely to avoid it and thus to fail on your own terms.

But wait. This is not about escaping from what is, for most people, the inevitability of mediocrity. This is about how to get there faster and more efficiently

– that is, by plan. And keep in mind that becoming mediocre is something that almost everyone you know (and some you don't) can help you achieve. If you did want to succeed, instead of lolling around in mediocrity, you would suffer not only being alone in your quest, but you would suffer the derision of the majority – who speak from the strength of numbers. The question is, how can you get there – to the depth of mediocrity – before they do?

An elusive lesson may come from the French playwright Beaumarchais who, in his play, *The Marriage of Figaro* (1784), said,

> "*If you are mediocre and you grovel, you shall succeed.*"

First Lesson:

Be **arrogant** in your mediocrity!

I say, avoid groveling. Wear your mediocrity like a cloak of honor. Be arrogant in your mediocrity. Be superior, celebrate! Let people suffer the ruthlessness of your determination to be mediocre! You have to be *more* mediocre than your thousands of competitors. *More* mediocre than your colleagues, than your family, more mediocre than your friends. This means avoiding any success that might come from apologizing in any way for your mediocrity. Be the one-eyed king in the kingdom of blind people.

For many years in Australian business circles, the implicit code of your mates was that outperforming them was okay only if it happened by accident. But if you were trying to become excellent on purpose, you would be scorned (the "tall poppy" syndrome – a metaphor for cutting people who intend to be better than you are off at the knees). Did the Australian business community get this from us? There are still vestiges of that attitude in America, especially within organizations that are themselves mediocre.

Avoid the scorn of success. Be no more ambitious than the next fellow. And, if some success does come your way, be embarrassed by the way it happened upon you in spite of your best intentions … to be a "good mate."

> *Marie was a modest lady. She was very bright, more capable even, than some of the fellow employees in her department. Even than some of her superiors in the organization. But she deferred to them, something she somehow learned growing up. She wanted to avoid rocking the boat in any way. She wanted to be as invisible and anonymous as possible, never to be the source of controversy or the center of attention. Her immediate boss liked her for her attitude of silent servitude, because he was just like her. You know, getting along with everyone. They were both well-liked by their peers. They both failed, together, as the company slowly slipped into oblivion.*

The lesson? She had no *plan* for failing. Nor did the company. Shameful.

To fail by default – for example, by being mediocre – is even more embarrassing than succeeding by default, i.e., by luck. **If you're going to do it, do it with great fanfare and aplomb.** Otherwise you won't get credit for it. And what kind of life would that be?

D'Israeli wrote:

> *"...it is a wretched taste to be gratified with mediocrity when the excellent lies before us."*

Well, how wrong could he be? In a democracy, taste lies with the majority of people. And if people in such overwhelming numbers are gratified with their mediocrity, who is he to pretend to be above the crowd? Be wary of "excellence." It will bring you nothing but trouble and travail. Far better to take the easy path. Don't take Robert Frost's "path less taken." Get on the one with the deepest rut. Outdo your fellow-travelers on the path to mediocrity. Elevate your mediocrity to the most superior form of life, and of your performance at work. This will not only make you very popular, but it will accelerate your failure. Be a role model for the mediocre.

Second Lesson:
Be a role model for the mediocre.

Everyone knows that a leader, by definition, is a person who has "followers." Which only means that it is the mediocre followers who make leaders successful – or not – in their bizarre quests. Flex your muscles. That's where the power lies – with the mediocre. Be their champion.

The managers and executives who fail, whether out of laziness, indifference, or sheer incompetence, are the ones who preferred the path most taken: the easy path, the path worn down by millions – just like them!

There cannot be any real stigma attached to failure, of course, if "everybody" is doing it. That's the beauty of mediocrity. Stick with the crowd. They'll take you there with minimum effort. With a little more effort on your part, you'll get there afore 'em.

Here's the bottom-line:

- If you need to be liked, you will fail. Easy enough.
- If you always need to be approved of, you will fail. Be obsequious.
- If you need to go where everyone else is going, you will fail. Go with the flow.
- If you are unwilling or unable to pay the price to succeed, you will fail. If success isn't free or at least cheap, don't buy it. Argue for "balance."
- If you hang out with mediocrities, you will fail. But get them to hang out with you. Be their exemplar.
- If you don't know the difference between good advice and bad advice, you will fail. Accelerate your journey: be a raving fan for bad advice.

There you have it. Six of the "thirty-six habits" (or whatever) for achieving mediocrity.

Albert Einstein once observed,

> "*Great spirits have always found violent opposition from mediocrities.*"

Well, okay. But where would Einstein's opposition have come from without all of those "mediocrities"?

Take solace and validation from Somerset Maugham's observation:

See also: Ray Bennett, *The Underachiever's Manifesto* (Chronicle Books, 2006)

"Only a mediocre person is always at his best."

All you have to do is be more mediocre than they are, at their own game.

Recipe #3

How to Develop Your Own Incompetence

Many of those executives who play the game but fail may be better prepared for failing than you are and may therefore have an advantage. So first, let's level the playing field.

Those executives better prepared for failure may have been more incompetent at the outset to perform their roles. If they have this advantage over you, it means you may have to consciously develop and expand your existing *incompetencies* in order to fail in your role, with more flair and dispatch, while they fail pitifully, never quite knowing why.

C. S. Lewis suggested that

> *"The safest road to Hell is the gradual one ..."*

But, hey, you're not going to live forever. You've got to move things along if you are going to fail heroically in your own lifetime.

Here's a secret of value. It's a secret because others apparently don't know about it: The fact is that

First Lesson:
Many appointed to high positions are not competent in those roles.

many, if not most, of the people who get appointed to high level management or executive roles are not competent to perform in that role.

But, you're asking yourself, Then, how DID they get there? One way is by traversing diverse and irrational paths to that position. For instance …

- Some had parents who wanted a family member to carry on. Those executives weren't interviewed for the position. They were herded into it.
- Others relied on the "good old boys" network. Often it's because the "good old boys" figured they would be rewarded if they put Joe in the power seat. Known smilingly as inside "politics."
- Sometimes the power brokers just decide "it's time for a change." It's the change that's important, not the qualifications of the person.
- Sometimes they get chosen because they aren't troublesome. It's okay if the new executive rocks the boat. As long as it isn't their boat. Best choice: someone who rocks *no* one's boat.
- Sometimes it's impossible to know just why someone was promoted. Which usually means that the person who got put into that role is clueless, also.

Napoleon, whose "success paradigm" worked well indeed – until it failed rather spectacularly – said he didn't want "competent" field generals. He wanted "lucky" ones. Apparently he failed at that. "Luck" works in both directions. Make sure you enlist it in your cause to get on the down side.

The fact is, people get themselves cast in roles they are incompetent to perform. They've never been in that particular role before. How they will perform in that role can't be known for sure until after they're in it. So the odds are that you will get cast in a role where you can put your incompetence to work. And, you have "luck" on your side. Since many more people fail than succeed, and since "luck" plays a significant part in both, it's simply more likely that you will "get lucky" and *fail.*

You may have to offset the contributions of "good" luck by diligently honing your incompetencies. You can always fail by default, of course, like most others. But **if you want to exhibit integrity and fail by a successful strategy for doing so, you may have to work at developing the incompetencies required**, no matter what the circumstances.

> *There was this guy – we'll call him Charlie – who wanted in the worst way to be "the boss." And he felt sure he deserved the role. Even his mother told him so. Well, as it turned out, he was selected, not because he was especially qualified in any clear way, but because he was, in the eyes of those who selected him, the* ***least worst*** *candidate for the role.*
>
> *So he eagerly took the role on – surrounded as he was with people who had no better sense than to select him. They believed that they were superior simply because they agreed on putting Charlie in charge. That way, they were doing him a favor. Of course, they wanted favors in return. Primarily, they intended that Charlie would therefore overlook* ***their*** *incompetencies. This worked, given his belief that their choice of him meant they were really smart people. And they all lived unhappily, for a short time after.*

This is standard operating procedure in mediocre organizations. Being chosen by or being surrounded by incompetent people is a method that almost guarantees your own incompetence. **Incompetent people prefer the company of other incompetent people – there is strength and justification in numbers.**

How does all of this work when things are just ducky? Well, you have to work at it to fail in "good" times. Any oaf can fail in "bad" times. As paradoxical as it may seem, you have to make your incompetencies more obvious in "good" times. (Interesting how the tough times swell the ranks of failed managers and executives faster than the easy times do. It's just that much harder to fail when things are going well.) You have to develop your incompetencies so that you can fail in spite of the upward trend. Don't wait around for the circumstances to turn you into a failure. To be successful at failing on purpose, practice when times are good.

Second Lesson:
Practice at failing when times are good.

Here are a couple of thoughts to ponder:

Peter Drucker said,

> *"So much of what we call management consists in making it difficult for people to work."*

Practice *those* management principles daily.

Or, this one:

> *A corporation board was to deliberate on the qualifications for a new department head. The board chairman opened the meeting by saying, "Let's remember that we want someone who is not too conservative and not too radical. In other words, we want somebody just mediocre."*

That somebody could be…you!

As you can see, lots of people in high places are ready, willing, and able to help you get on and stay on this path. Just make sure they see your mediocrity clearly. You don't want to *appear* to be incompetent. You want to appear to be sincerely applying yourself. Work hard, put in long hours, be no real threat to anybody by accomplishing something, and attribute your shortcomings to overwork. This is how you play that game.

Fake it. Until you arrive at the level where the "Peter Principle" takes over and it becomes obvious to everyone that you haven't got what it takes. Make your plan work.

A few people are out there having a go at developing their competencies with real fervor. Be as diligent at developing your incompetencies as they are. It's a tougher path to take, because most people are relatively incompetent by default, and therefore it's hard to stand out in the crowd. It's the default part you have to overcome. Even if you make failure your purpose in life, you could still get lucky and succeed in spite of yourself. Don't let this happen, no matter how appealing it might be in your weaker moments to be successful in spite of yourself. Fail by design. You want people to say, "He did that!"

Not, "That just sort of happened to him."

Now, here's a cage-rattling way of looking at it that will endear you to your peers: it takes as much competence to fail as it does to succeed. Just at different things. Surely it has occurred to you that a kid has to be competent at ways of not doing well in school. These ways have to be practiced until they become habits. It takes habits to drive failure just as much as it takes habits to drive success.

Most people believe that you succeed by intention, but that you fail through no fault of your own. By default. They're wrong, of course. And here's where you can make your mark – by showing others how you failed, through your competencies for doing so.

There's a lot of swaggering and chest-thumping going on these days when someone happens to be successful. Yet we know that more than half of it going either way is sheer luck. Those who have some minor success don't want to share the spotlight with Lady Luck. So they take full credit for their success. It's only when you can take full credit for your failures that you'll be on solid ground. Lead the way to this revelation. People will think you're crazy. But what historical figure who changed the way people saw truth or beauty was *not* considered crazy?

That's right. Your mission is a heroic one. Don't see it that way? Well, you'll likely fail at it, then.

Third Lesson:

A key secret for how to fail is: **Avoid** succeeding.

A key secret for how to fail is: *Avoid succeeding.* After all, most people who succeed do so in the same way as most people who fail. By default. Avoid succeeding by default, and you're a cinch.

Still, failing on purpose is much more challenging than it first appears to be. You remember Sun-tzu's *The Art of War*. Offered there are all sorts of stratagems for success. So you have to think about how you can turn those stratagems on their head.

For example, at one point, he suggests …

> *"Even though you are competent, appear to be incompetent."*

Practice turning these stratagems for success on their head. For instance: **Even though you are incompetent, appear to be competent.** You'll be detected.

Most people feel no responsibility for their own incompetencies. The mentality of mediocre organizations is that someone higher up can compensate for those at the bottom. If your intention is to fail on purpose, you don't want a bunch of busybodies trying to reform you. If the permissiveness of an environment that tolerates incompetence leaks into your organization and settles in as part of its culture, your increasing incompetencies will go unnoticed. You're probably familiar with "The Peter Principle" (mentioned earlier) – that, "in a hierarchy, every manager tends to rise to his level of total incompetence."

"The Peter Principle" means that, like thousands of others, it may be inevitable that you will achieve failure eventually. **But you want to develop your incompetencies so you can get there faster** and, unlike those who ride the waves, with purpose and aplomb.

One last thought. Not an unimportant one. There are basically two kinds of incompetence. One lies in failing to imagine that everything could probably be done better, and then inventing the tools or techniques – the competencies required – for doing so. The other, more mundane kind of incompetence lies in simply being incapable of carrying out the tasks before you even though the necessary tools and techniques *are* available. *You* have to master **both** kinds of incompetence to fail on purpose and with aplomb.

This illustration comes from Peter Dunne's turn-of-the-century character, Mr. Dooley:

> *Mr. Hennessy once asked Mr. Dooley if he thought all of our accumulated knowledge had much to do with progress in the world.*
>
> *Well," Mr. Dooley replied, "do you think it is the mill that makes the water run?"*

If the lesson in that comes to you quickly, **then you're a poor candidate for expeditious failure.** In that case, it just means that you'll have to work harder at it.

Recipe #4

How to Nourish Incompetence in Others

Competence seems so robust and even indestructible, compared to incompetence. By contrast, incompetence seems somewhat tenuous, fragile, more readily eliminated or changeable. That's probably one reason why, in typical organizations, incompetence is protected and overlooked.

This is a form of "nourishment."

Competence may be expected at some level. But when you don't get what is expected in a culture in which incompetence is treated like a protected species, people complain about it in general. Little, if anything, is ever done about it. That would require someone to name names. To speak the truth to another person's face. And everybody knows *that*, if not actually discourteous, it is certainly not the way things work. Decorum before performance.

So, again, you're up against it. You need to nourish a condition in others that fits our declining standards and is therefore going to be nourished by the culture of the organization you work in. This requires some ingenuity. Some cunning and cageyness on your part.

We have established in these first four chapters of *How Executives Fail* that you live in a land where incompetence reigns. It's likely, for example, that the costs of dealing with, and compensating for, the ever-increasing flood of incompetence is what actually buoys our economy.

First Lesson:
Incompetence buoys our economy.

So if you're going to make your mark here, you have to outdo this well-nigh universal indulgence of incompetence – by choosing your incompetencies, and by working to nourish this in others.

You have to do this. You need to be surrounded by incompetent people in order to fail expeditiously and definitively. The level of incompetence in your organization may be sufficient for other managers and executives to fail by default. But to fail on purpose means you have no choice but to up the ante – the "ante," in this case, being the breadth and depth of incompetence by which you surround yourself. You *have to* actively nourish it.

It may seem a bit bizarre to think about or to practice nourishing *incompetence*. But parents do it regularly. Bosses do it daily. It may not be their intention to nourish others' incompetencies, but the outcome is the same no matter how inadvertent or unintentional. Your advantage lies not in doing what they do. That seems to be a la mode. **Your advantage lies in nourishing others' incompetencies *intentionally.***

The indispensable prerequisite for implementing this recipe for failure is that you are yourself short of the competence called for by your role. That's easy enough – SOP (standard operating procedure) in most mediocre organizations. If you pick your own bosses carefully, they'll help. Chances are they are themselves short of being fully competent in their own roles, so they will appreciate the fact that you are even less competent than they are. And they will encourage the gap between you so that they look good by comparison and can blame you for any performance shortfalls for which they might otherwise be responsible.

> *Jack was one of those guys that everybody liked when he interviewed at Bogus Corporation. He was easy-going, easy to talk to. A couple of the people who interviewed him pointed out that his background was lackluster, and they were hoping to get a real winner this time.*
>
> *But, as someone else commented, "Well, we couldn't hire someone who is really qualified for what we want. We can't pay at that level. We have to be satisfied with what we can get for what we are able to pay." They all agreed that they could "get along with him."*
>
> *Performance had never been a matter of high priority at Bogus. So Jack came on board. He got along well with his peers and his superiors, eventually rising to the executive ranks himself. He played golf with the owner. He saw a lot of inadequacies at the top level of management. But it didn't take him long to learn that blowing the whistle at Bogus was not something one did if one wanted to get a retirement package.*
>
> *So he did what was always done: He hired mediocre people. He praised their work if he liked them. His own incompetence thus got nourished. He never really had to think about it. It seemed "natural" to nourish the incompetence of those who worked with him.*

The obvious lesson is that **if you want to nourish your own or others' incompetence, the world we live in stands ready to help you;** friends, peers, the culture of your organization. But that's incompetence by default.

How many people have you known who have declared their intention to be incompetent? And yet most are, more or less. Real lesson to ponder: why *is* that? Use that to your advantage.

So what are some of the specific strategies and techniques for nourishing others' incompetencies?

First, feed yourself and others on the equivalent of junk food for the mind. This will clog the arteries. Speak junk. Hear junk. Do junk. This will contribute to the inability to think and to learn.

For the essential health of the organization, **what constitutes junk food? Anything that does not contribute to performance and growth in excellence.** In most organizations, that would be most of what passes for "communication" in and out of "meetings," which is where people congregate to add to the junk pile. Have lots of these. Permit people to meander, tell stories, and compete in the production of junk mind-food.

Two, you must be seen as the exemplar — that is, as the person who is living proof that it is admissible in your organization for people to be incompetent in high places. This will help you attract mediocre or otherwise incompetent additions to your organization. Those kinds of people want to get a "job" at a place where they are going to be actually rewarded for their incompetence. Make your place their place.

Three, help others find their comfort zone and make it impenetrable. Do everything you can to make them feel satisfied with themselves the way they are; be their role model for this kind of self-satisfaction. As Thomas Edison put it,

> *"Show me a thoroughly satisfied man – and I will show you a failure."*

Use this recipe.

Four, assume that no one has a choice but to be the way they are. Understand that there were circumstances that produced them about which they had no choice. That way, you will be shutting down the possibility that they might actually *choose* to be competent.

Five, you know intuitively that ignorance is a great aid in being liked. As Will Rogers once quipped,

> *"You know everybody is ignorant, only on different subjects."*

Make sure that you surround yourself with people who are ignorant on the same subjects as their peers. That way you can expect to have a "team" with great morale.

Six, surround yourself with sycophants. A sycophant is a "servile flatterer." You need them to keep you on the path to failure. Realize that you must also *be* a sycophant. It will help your boss help you to fail.

Seven, encourage your people to feed off of their appreciation of themselves. If they can observe you feeding off of your own appreciation of yourself, they can see how it's done.

> Second Lesson:
>
> Serve these ten nourishing strategies often.

Eight, eliminate people who are in the learning mode. They're trouble-makers. Pal around with those who are in the knowing mode. It will help them if they can observe how closed-minded you are. Be arrogant – you already know what you need to know.

Nine, Use pop psychology in your relationships with your people. Be quick to use the current buzz-words in interpreting their feelings. Such as, "I can understand why you feel burned-out. You've been working too hard." Encourage them to have personal problems and to let their work be negatively affected by those personal problems. Deal with them on a psychological level – never in terms of real performance and real performance measures. You will nourish their incompetence if they can see how *your* personal feelings and personal problems get in the way of *your* performance.

Indulgence makes the heart grow fonder, and causes people's performance to diminish over time. Pretend you like them, and that your approval of them is what really counts. **If they take their destiny in their own hands, you are lost. Their destiny needs to be in your hands.** Treat them as you would dependent children or helpless victims. And get your boss to treat you the same way.

And, **ten**, assume that caring about people – about putting people first – is all about indulging them. Attend to their whims and their petty concerns. Encourage them to be depressed or to feel angry or mistreated. Anything to keep them from crawling out of their holes by becoming more competent.

These are strategies that work. Truer words were never spoken as those by William Proxmire about the Chrysler bailout in 1979. Proxmire lamented,

> *"Are we going to guarantee businessmen against their own incompetence?"*

Yes. That's exactly what you need to do to nourish incompetence in others.

Substitute "this organization" for "town" in this observation from Mark Twain's H*uckleberry Finn* and you'll see the value of widespread incompetence:

> *"Hain't we got all the fools in town on our side? And ain't that a big enough majority in any town?"*

Nourish incompetence until it becomes a critical mass. That engine will guarantee your success at failure.

Recipe #5

How to Be the Measure of All Things

Being appointed an "executive" seems to unleash people's egos. In order to complete the unsure journey of getting there, they had to pretend that they knew everything. When they arrive in the seat of power, they no longer have to pretend, they can now assume they really do know everything.

First Lesson:
When you become an executive, you really do know everything.

Who is going to challenge them? Not you. Certainly not their peers.

Their peers are unleashed and out of control in the same way. Sometimes there is rancor in the upper reaches of the organization. That's because it's tricky to try to get more than two over-inflated egos in the same room at the same time. The struggle is always about whose "reality" will prevail? There is no executive suite that is not politicized. Deal-making and coalitions are the order of the day — every day. Most executives don't know what they're doing any more than the rest of us do. But, with enough power, it will seem to them that they have been enfranchised to pronounce what's what and why.

We raise our children to revel in being the center of the universe. We seem to believe that individualism and egotism are the same thing. Such children are the masters of all they survey. The way they see the world is the way the world *is*. A tantrum will punctuate the dominance of their view of the world over any reality they might come up against … until they meet up with other children who have been raised the same way.

At the heart of this mental disorder is the conviction that as an executive it is now safe to assume that one is the measure of all things – that all of what one knows and believes has now been recognized as "the truth." That one's view of the world is somehow omniscient. **That one has become the measure of the world, rather than the other way around.** It's a disease. Apparently a very contagious one.

Then it becomes like a precursor to the executive suite. A world of politicking and coalitions. Maybe the condition of executive-ness is a regression to that childhood sense of power and right. Maybe not. Whatever its source, it seems almost inescapable. Being an "executive" is an ego trip for most who assume that mantle.

Back in 1955, it was suggested in *Look* magazine that,

> *"Egotism is the anesthetic that dulls the pain of stupidity."*

That's worth thinking about. Maybe it's not entirely true, but surely you have known people who fit the mold. It seems sometimes that the stupider people are, the more likely it is that they will be egotistical. Again, have you ever encountered this in others? In yourself?

It's easy to see this disease in other people, but it's difficult to see it in oneself. This kind of *egomania* is seeing something in ourselves others cannot see. (Alexander "the Great" – and that was his idea – was certain he was a god. There is probably nothing more like god on earth than a top executive on his or her perch.)

When you measure all others by yourself, and all ideas by your own, and all views of reality by your own private view of reality, you're bound to see in yourself what others cannot see. The *lesson* here is clear: If you set yourself up as the measure of all things, and if others don't knock you off your throne, reality inevitably will. The broader, deeper, and more disdainful your egomania, the quicker and the more glorious will be your failure.

A short story:

> *Mary Ellen was justifiably proud of her career, which had brought her from the lower reaches of the company to its upper echelon over the past twenty years. She had worked hard and long suffering fools all along the way. She was tired of being humble.*
>
> *Surely she was chosen because she was more knowledgeable and more prescient than anyone else who might have been considered for her position. She was exuberant. At last she could be herself, and change things in the way they ought to be.*
>
> *She began paying back some of her now-peers for what she considered to be past offenses. Unable to coalesce power around herself, she turned to the trendiest new ideas and management techniques as a way to be more powerful. She used "participative management" as a way of demonstrating her superiority. She pretended to "care" about people so that they might be more willing to bust their humps for her. Her idea about*

"servant leadership" was that it was a good way to clear away others' resistance to her plans.

Feeling besieged because she didn't want to play executive-suite politics left her without much of a constituency. When her failures became obvious, no one wept.

Lord Acton's famous lines: **Power corrupts, and absolute power corrupts absolutely** are demonstrated here. Be like Mary Ellen – as good an example as anyone has ever seen of the truth of that observation.

The business press panders to egomaniacs. The business press understands the egomaniac market. This business press of ours (run largely by egotists, and always your ally on the slippery slope to failure) targets those people who are willing to pay big bucks for any help they can get on their own ego trip.

"Fairy dust" – ideas and techniques you buy that you can sprinkle over people and then the world will be the way you want it to be – appeals to egotists, because they assume they were the ones who thought of it in the first place. They don't access the media to learn anything. They do so to confirm what they already know. Every editor is aware of this.

Second Lesson:
To be a world-class egomaniac you must force the world into your view of it.

As the French savant Joubert quipped,

> *"What can you possibly add to a mind that's full, especially one that's full of itself?"*

To be a world-class egomaniac, you must invariably try to force the world into your conception of it. You may feel indignant when that doesn't work. You may occasionally get depressed by the unfairness of reality. But that's the personal price you have to pay to be the measure of all things.

Assume that others and the continuation of this world depend utterly upon you. Assume, as an old saying goes, that

> *"If you hadn't been born, people would have wondered why."*

Compliment others openly when they defer to you and your over-weaning omniscience. Encourage them to be awed by your posture – proving that you already knew everything worth knowing well before they were even born. Embarrass them whenever they presume to say something that you might not have known.

Be vocal about your belief that people should be more assertive and figure things out for themselves. But make it apparent to them at every opportunity that, compared to you, they are mental midgets. If they claim experience, come up with a plausible reason why they would be wrong to be guided by their trivial experience – compared to yours. Lord it over them. After all, that's why you were chosen for the lordship role.

You have perhaps very cleverly detected that there's a catch here. There is. The catch is that if you don't appear to have a big enough ego, you may not be considered executive material – a role you have to get cast in before you can legitimately fail in it.

Easily circumvented. Letting your superiors be the measure of all things will garner their favor. Then, when you have been cast in the role, bring to bear the worst of all the egomaniacs you've had to kiss-up-to on your way up. Once in the role, be prepared to let your ego ride roughshod over everything and everybody. Your time has come to be the measure of all things. Let no one doubt that.

The more irritating you are to your peers, the sooner they will want to be rid of you. To paraphrase Robert Frost,

> *Perform the kind of egotism the other executives' egotism can't put up with.*

If that's too easy, aim for being the all-time master at being the measure of all things — especially of *them.* Never be caught without a way of trumping everyone else's input.

If you discover that isn't working – simply because your peers put up with your egotism as long as you put up with theirs – take solace in the old adage that says,

> *Egotism is the kind of disease where the patient feels okay, but his organization is sick.*

You have to make a choice. As Frank Lloyd Wright explained himself,

> *"I had to choose between honest arrogance and hypocritical humility."*

Choose wisely. Otherwise you may succeed in spite of yourself. Most of those who succeed do so in spite of themselves. You have to be vigilant at all times to avoid the pitfalls of success.

Remember this: People succeed by avoiding failure. In the same way, people fail by avoiding success. **Being the one who is always right is a great recipe for doing that.**

Recipe #6

How to Maintain Your Gullibility

Gull is an interesting word. To "gull" originally meant to dupe, or trick, or deceive. A gullible person is therefore a person who is easily cheated or duped. But we're looking at a characteristic of being human. As you probably well know by now, it takes two or more people to create a human truth: one to utter it, another to believe it. That's just the way it works. There are always consequences – good or bad.

Saying "Good job!" to another person who believes it is an example. If he does, he may think you're "gulling" him. If he doesn't, then he just "gulled" you. This is frequently the case in organizations. The point is you will always be second-guessed.

So let's face it. We're all gullible – some more so, some less so. We have a very low threshold for hearing and seeing what we are ready, willing, and able to believe. We have a very high threshold for hearing or seeing what may be contrary to what we already believe. Everyone has "hot buttons." Those are inclinations to believe certain things and not other things. Other people push our hot buttons. That's how we get "gulled."

The British philosopher Bertrand Russell described our susceptibilities – or our credulousness – in the following way. Every person, he wrote, wherever that person goes,

> *"... is encompassed by a cloud of comforting convictions, which move with him like flies on a summer day."*

Other people, noticing these obvious hot buttons, assume it is in their best interest to add flies to the "cloud" – and thus add to the comfort of those convictions. In other words, it's easy to believe what you are already predisposed to believe, no matter how reliable its source. This is what makes it easy for the people who flock around you to say or do only those things you will find pleasing, or easily believed. "Toadying" takes two.

First Lesson:

Toadying takes two.

Children have to be credulous. Otherwise they wouldn't learn anything. What they are told may be harmful to their long-term health and welfare. That remains the case for us all of our lives. The point of growing up is to be able to discern what's worth knowing – given your destination in life. If you don't have a destination, you remain as credulous as a child, flitting here and there trying to "find" yourself.

On the other hand, if you can become omniscient overnight by being appointed the boss, you now have a different problem. Your problem now is avoiding hearing or seeing something that is not consistent with what you already know.

Carl, the top executive, was having lunch with Don, a subordinate, but one he had known for a long time.

Most people who fail assume by the time they are thirteen years old or so that they already know what they need to know for the rest of their lives. **You have to consciously raise this to an art form.** This must be your strategy, not your flaw.

"Don," Carl said, "I want you to level with me. Why is it that I'm the last person in the company to learn that we have serious problems in engineering, or in shipping, or wherever? I tell my people, 'You can tell me what you see is going on. Even if it's bad news, I can take it.' "

Don replies, "Yes, that's what you've always told me."

Carl continues, "If there's a problem somewhere, I want to know about it, so we can find out who's to blame."

"Maybe," Don muses quietly, "that's part of the problem. After all, who wants to be the one who catches hell–or the one who rats on the offender?"

"But, by damn, we're all obligated to identify the incompetents in this organization so we can root them out!" Carl exclaimed.

"Well," Don replied, "I remember how you disagreed with Sue's assessment of our marketing problem. As I recall, you told her in so many words that she was wrong, given your superior experience about such things. Can you shut people down but expect them to open up?"

"Agghh, Don, that's too much like modern bullshit to me. We've all got a job to do, and part of it is dealing with reality rather than opinions."

"Whose?"

"Whose what?"

"Whose reality? Yours or theirs?"

"It's the same thing. Reality is reality."

"It is if you're the big boss. But not when the boss's approval of you hangs on it. For example, there are some people out there who think the main problem is you. How do you feel about that?"

"Well," Carl said, eyeing Don carefully, "they would be wrong, of course. And you know it."

"Yep," Don replied, "I do."

To whom is the big boss accountable? When was the last time you saw a big boss fire himself or herself for reasons of incompetence? Why does that never happen? But Carl is failing by default. *You* have to have the kind of class that enables you to raise your self-gullibility to the heights.

You may remember the Aesop fable about the rats and the cat. The rats were discussing their vulnerability because they couldn't hear the cat coming. Much discussion. Ending with the question,

"Agreed. We should put a bell on the cat's neck so we can hear it coming. But who is going to bell the cat?"

Corollary: Who is going to get in the line of fire by telling you what's wrong with *you*? Keep it that way.

For those who are gullible – or need to be more gullible – there are two categories of predators to whom you need to open your mind and your heart.

One category: Those who seek to sell you something by telling you what you can readily believe – you know, consultants, magazine and book editors, etc. The business press is largely a support industry for handicapped people.

The other category: Those who seek to gain your favor, or avoid your displeasure, by slyly confirming your beliefs, prejudices, and perspectives – you know, subordinates, talented suck-ups, peers who are fearful of your power, fans, etc.

As the humorist Josh Billings once said,

> *"It is better to know nothing than to know what ain't so."*

But who's going to tell you? Especially if what isn't so is the image you have of yourself? Not your predators. It was in the 1932 movie *Poppy* that W. C. Fields quipped,

> *"Never give a sucker an even break."*

This is the M.O. for predators. **Make your predators successful!**

Not yet convinced? Samuel Butler remarked,

> *"From a worldly point of view, there is no mistake so great as that of always being right."*

Take the tip. *Always* be right.

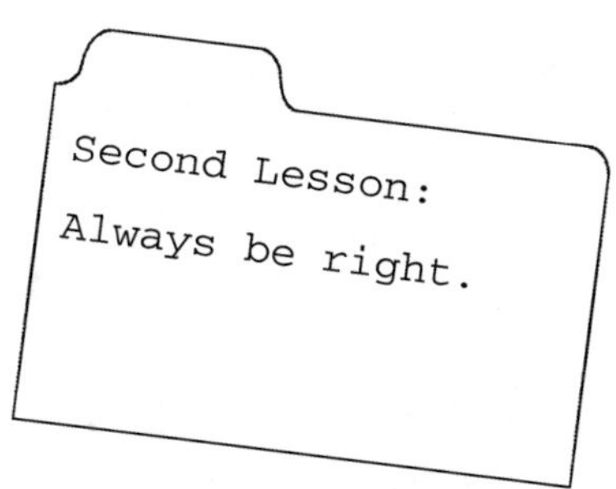

And as you develop and hone your competencies for failing, always remember the old adage,

> *The person who thinks he knows everything is irritating to those of us who do.*

The more you can irritate others in this way, the faster you will fail. Think on the possibilities.

Recipe #7

How to Be Tolerant of Those Who Can't ... Or Won't

We've all been told that tolerance is a virtue. But it all depends on what you are trying to accomplish. Doesn't it? An athlete or a musician who is too tolerant of his or her last performance is never going to make it to the top. A rock climber who is too tolerant of his or her carelessness last time on the cliff may end up being an ex-climber.

Seems that tolerance has its uses. But it also seems that *intolerance* has its uses.

First Lesson:

Be infinitely tolerant of your shortfalls.

We may never have heard that intolerance is a virtue. But when tolerance becomes another term for incompetence or indifference, you may be forgiving yourself – or others – for being on the wrong path. Unless, of course, the path you want to be on is the path that takes you to your failure. In that case, simply persist in trashing yourself and others by being infinitely tolerant of your – and their – shortfalls.

Here's a story that tells the story:

> *Joe was an eager young manager who tolerated the shortfalls and the miscues of his subordinates. He probably got that idea for how to manage from some "New Age" seminar – you know, about how to be successful by being a nice guy. Anyway, he was exceedingly tolerant of his subordinates' failures to perform as required. There always seemed to be a good reason. And they, in turn, reciprocated by tolerating his shortfalls and miscues as their boss.*
>
> *He was personable, likeable, and Oh! so sincere. He had grown up around friends, teachers, and his own prior bosses, who were tolerant of his poor performance, his failures to live up to his promises and expectations. So that way of "managing" made total good sense to him. After all, there were always good reasons for not coming through. Naturally, this meant that he had to forgive his own failures to live up to his own expectations.*
>
> *He was well-liked, especially by those around him who were themselves indifferent. So, since birds of a feather flock together, he attracted those who just sort of got by. And he was attracted to them. All because he was tolerant of poor performance–his own and thus theirs.*

The lesson here is simple enough. The more tolerance you have for your own poor performance, the more tolerance you will have for others' incompetencies and failures to perform. And the more tolerant (gullible?) you will be for excuses offered for failures to perform. So be tolerant of your own shortfalls, and those who think like you do will gather to be around you and each other. They'll help you to fail.

No matter how diligently you strategize your own failure, you won't get the credit for it if it looks like it was the other people around you who did you in. You not only want to fail with gusto and acumen, you have to *appear* to be wholly responsible for your own failure, as Gracian (the 17th-century philosopher) advised the leaders of his day–and of ours. That may mean you must *appear* to be intolerant of others' under-performance, but appear *not* to be intolerant of your own. Or is that just the political mantra of the typical manager?

There's a pitfall here, though. A paradox. You'll attract the kind of people who are tolerant of your incompetencies and their own. **But you have to make sure that they don't get the credit for your failure.** This means that their contributions to your failure have to be invisible, never acknowledged, even though indispensable.

Some unknown wag put it this way:

> *"The trouble with being tolerant is that people will think you don't understand the problem."*

Perfect! And, as a recipe for failing, certainly not much of a stretch for most executives.

Here are some other tips for making indiscriminate tolerance work for you:

- Like the piano tuner who is called on stage to tune the piano during the orchestra's performance, be sure to come on board at your organization when everyone is thoroughly engaged in the score (the culture) they were following before you got there. Be tolerant of their old ways to ensure that they don't have to change either their ways of thinking or their ways of doing.

- Make sure that the people who are going to be working with you all have "tenure." That is, that you have no choice but to have them on your staff. And that you can't eliminate them or even try to change them, because they are there under a sort of grandfather clause. It will help if their comfort zones are as protected as the habitats of endangered species are protected. That being so, it's up to them whether to take you seriously or not, depending on how guaranteed their positions are. So be judicious and milk this for all it's worth.

Everyone knows that if you had the prerogative to choose people who might make you "successful," there's the barest possibility it might happen, thus interfering with your trip to failure. **Be indiscriminately tolerant of those who have a comfort zone guaranteed by the pre-existing culture.**

- The ancient Greek wisdom had it right:

  "You cannot confer a benefit on an unwilling person."

  Here you may need to be tolerant of their unwillingness. If you had your way, their comfort zones would be in jeopardy, and then they would in all likelihood be willing to conspire to take you down. But then it would look like it was your fault for not being tolerant of their unwillingness.

- And here's a clincher: If you are tolerant enough of your own stupidity to believe that you have the kind of superhuman powers that would enable you to change people against their will (what's implied when the "experts" talk about such myths as "motivation"), then you've got things in place for optimizing the likelihood of your failure.

In short, as the old saying goes,

"You can't make a silk purse out of a sow's ear."

This works to your advantage. If "sow's ears" are what you need to fail superbly, start with them, and proceed with tolerance. No expert ever suggested that you could make a sow's ear out of a silk purse. So make sure you don't have too many "silk purses" hanging around. You can't change them, and they will impede your mission.

Second Lesson: Start with sow's ears and proceed with tolerance.

When people don't perform as required or as promised, there are two possible reasons. Either they can't. Or they won't. You've observed this in yourself. Here the larger culture is going to work to your advantage. Because the assumption about under-performance is not that a person "won't." It is that he or she "can't." If you happen to perform in a way that might jeopardize your mission to fail, others will attribute it to your inability to do otherwise. Don't let your ego get in the way here. Accept others' judgment that you are just in over your head. They'll forgive you for that. But not for failing on purpose. Be tolerant of others' abject stupidity on this score. Assume you can't – assume that no one can – *choose* not to perform as required.

Tolerance may not encourage people to make mistakes. But it tells them it is okay to make mistakes if they can come up with a plausible excuse. So the more tolerant you are, the more mistakes people will assume that they can make and still be in good stead.

Be tolerant of laziness in yourself or in others, and you'll get more of it. Be tolerant of incompetence in yourself and others, and you'll get more of that. Incompetence breeds incompetence.

If your plumber botches his work, be tolerant. He "tried." If your brain surgeon botches his work on you, be tolerant. He may have done his "best." See how easy it is to get by with poor performance? Americans have notoriously been tolerant of shoddy products and shoddy service. That's why we have had so much of it. But to fail on purpose means you have to *appear* to hold yourself and others to high standards of performance while being tolerant under the table of under-performance. Otherwise, you'll look like every other cluck who's failed.

Do the opposite of what Patton did. Inherit the worst staffers you can imagine. If you can't do that, choose people who aren't competent to perform in the roles you've cast them in. Be tolerant of their poor performance, and you'll get more of it.

As the writer Somerset Maugham put it:

> *"Tolerance is only another name for indifference."*

Does that ring a bell? Indifference is easy!

Herbert Samuel wrote,

> *"It is easy to be tolerant of the principles of other people if you have none of your own."*

Secret revealed. If you want to fail by design, either have no principles of your own, or be careful not to act on them.

***Tolerance* of sloth, incompetence, or under-engagement, whether those characteristics are yours or others', will provide all kinds of productive forces to ensure your failure.**

Recipe #8

How to Get Addicted

Everyone is addicted – just in different ways – to different things. The key here is getting yourself deeply addicted to the wrong things. People who do not fail on purpose are under the control of addictions they didn't know they had. It's as if they were on a default setting. Whatever happens is what happens.

First Lesson:
Choose addictions that propel you to failure.

This is a careless and irresponsible way to live. Choosing not to be addicted is not an option for you. Your challenge is to select and nurture those addictions that propel you on your chosen path toward expedient and intentional failure, of which you can be proud. There is no recognition for failing by default – only a, "Too bad. Wonder how *that* happened?"

You could get addicted to the popular things – like alcohol, drugs, tobacco, self. They'll help you to fail, for sure. The assumption, though, is that people are *victims* of these commonplace addictions. And that won't do. If you're going to fail on purpose, it has to be seen as *your* achievement. Not the achievement of the alcohol or the other obsessions that push you and pull you in spite of yourself.

What you're going to learn here is how to get addicted to uncommon things – like deference, power, and money. Like basking in the glow of the adoration and blind faith of some subordinates, who may themselves be clueless, and which others might perceive as kissing-up. Like the delusions that warm your heart when you look in the mirror. Such as your need to be liked well beyond your likeability.

Let's meet Tom:

Tom was one of those people who always looked forward to every workday morning, to driving off to work, and of settling into his office for the day. The main reason is that he didn't feel fully appreciated at home by his wife and children. Compared to his life at work, they always seemed to bring him down. They didn't seem to realize how important he was. How indispensable. How utterly superior he was. The way his subordinates treated him provided him always with the warmth of their deference to him in all matters.

Going home was a different world. His children treated him with signs of disrespect. His wife at times seemed to just tolerate him. At home he often sulked. Or was crabby and short-tempered. At work, it was pretty much the opposite. He was engaging, friendly, solicitous. At least as long as his subordinates treated him as he was certain he deserved to be treated.

In his eyes, he deserved to be looked up to, to be treated with deference and approval. He treated his own boss that way, and they seemed to get along really well, maybe because of that?

It never occurred to him to wonder if he was worthy. His subordinates assured him he was. "It's really great having you around," one of them would say. Or, "I really like working here, now that you're running things." But at home, and sometimes with his colleagues (but rarely) he felt unworthy.

He remembered one day as he came through the door, his wife said, "Hey, kids, dufus is home!"

One kid said, "Hi, dufus."

The others just glanced his way and went on with what they were doing. Tom figured that was not right, but was not his fault. There was something wrong with ***them****.*

He therefore always played for the applause of people who hoped to benefit by their adulation. In their private conversations, they spoke of him as an inconsequential wimp, an easy mark. This made them sometimes feel like whores. But they knew how to make him *happy. And that paid off. Just the way it was done in his organization.*

That's what addictions are for. They insulate you from reality. An addiction in play will keep reality at bay.

They creep up on us – our addictions. Just before they take over. People rarely choose an addiction. Unseen and insidious, they take over our lives, leading us by the hand wherever they want us to go. *Your* advantage lies in choosing. But, in choosing, to choose only those that will facilitate your failure. And consciously rejecting any that might lead you down the wrong path – toward success. As we just saw, Tom was addicted to his own delusions of superiority, coupled with his addiction to his subordinates' playing to his delusions – he has a combination that is sure to lead to failure. Nice work, Tom.

Here are some specifics that will help you to distinguish between the addictions you should and shouldn't choose:

- Ideas are addictive. There are those that will further your cause in failing on purpose. The more conventional those ideas are, the better, since conventional ideas will provide you with no competitive advantage. You've watched – or helped – others fail. Keep a list of "Best Practices" for failing hidden somewhere nearby.
- Like celebrity ideas, celebrity figures can be very addictive. That is, you can buy a book or an idea just because of its status.
- Get deeply addicted to yourself *as you are*. Carefully avoid learning anything that might lead you to change yourself.
- Cherish and defend your habits. If you don't let reality interfere, bad habits will serve you well in your quest to fail on purpose.
- Get addicted to always being "right," and to those who always agree with you.

A best-seller is a label used by book and magazine editors to provide an excuse for people who could never figure out for themselves whether they should "read" it or not. **Be led by people who want only your money or your unconditional approval and could care less whether you succeed or fail.** They're on your side.

- Get irretrievably addicted to those illusions about yourself that seem to fool others.
- Feed on the perks and pleasures that come from your position, especially your power over others, their dependence on you.
- Get addicted to others' dependence on your moods.
- Measure everything in material terms. Get addicted to money.
- Hang out with losers and "victims." Get addicted to their explanations.
- Surround yourself with people who have the same addictions you have.

"Addiction" is another word for *habit*, of course. So choose the kinds of habits you need in order to fail, and let them take over your life. Zelda Fitzgerald remarked in a 1923 interview,

> *"It's terrible to allow conventional habits to gain a hold on...* [a whole organization]."

Take the tip. The more conventional habits you and your organization can be addicted to, the more capable you will be of failing well ahead of schedule.

Let the habits you just happen to pick up along the way be the source of your inspiration. As Saint Augustine said,

> *"Habit, if not resisted, soon becomes necessity."*

What better definition of addiction could there be?

You probably haven't got what it takes (most of us don't) to guide your failure consciously and conscientiously. Let your addictions do it for you.

Here's how the poet W. H. Auden characterized the prognosis:

> *"All sin tends to be addictive, and the terminal point of addiction is what is called damnation."*

Well, maybe not damnation as such. Maybe just sinking into the slough of mediocrity, or actually failing in some more notable or humane way.

You want to get to where Queen Caroline got, when she was implored by her minions in the following verse:

> *"Most lofty boss, we thee implore*
> *to go away and mistreat us no more.*
> *But if that effort be too great,*
> *to go away at any rate."*

Not all addiction is "sinful" in the old-fashioned sense. Certainly unjustified pride is. And so is hubris, both of which are commonplace in the executive suites of our organizations. So is making pets or whores out of your subordinates. People can't get well in a sick organization. **Make sure your addictions nurture a sick organization.** That will help your cause. As you know well, being "the boss" is itself addictive. Play it for all you can.

Exit – that is, fail – with the blessings of those whom you abuse most with your multifarious addictions.

It's not just a matter of being a "toxic boss." You have to be toxic to yourself, thereby gaining failure momentum exponentially. If you are not poisonous to other people, they won't be "motivated" to get rid of you. And you need their help with your goal, which you can never reveal to them. If you did, they'd think you were merely crazy. And as you know, crazy people can't "fail." So you've got to grit your teeth and appear to be normal, while deviously and devilishly creating your notable failure.

Recipe #9

How to Be Reasonable

With all the "New Age" palaver swirling around you these days, it's likely you would assume right off that being "reasonable" is one way of ensuring your success as an executive. That popular bit of soft-headedness is not just wrong. It is 179 degrees off the mark.

First Lesson:
Just go with the flow.

Here again you could just float downstream on the river of faulty ideas. You would have lots of company. And lots of confirmation, making you feel like all these people couldn't be wrong. And therefore you couldn't possibly be wrong. But that would be shameful, to fail by default like so many of those others, by just going with the flow.

You've got to step up and keep your eye on the ball – failing on purpose and with your eyes wide open.

History 101:

> *The more people there are who believe something to be true, the more likely it is to be false.*

That's because success in this world doesn't depend on what people believe. It depends on your ability to think outside the box – that is, in a way contrary to how most of the mediocrities of the world think about things. So in order to avoid succeeding, you have to live in the platitudes most people live in. Don't struggle against the flow. Swim vigorously and competitively *with* the flow. Most people don't know they think inside a box. Be one of those. To repeat a basic premise for failing:

> *The way to fail is to avoid succeeding, just as the way to succeed is to avoid failing.*

There is a great launching pad for getting off and into this one. It comes from George Bernard Shaw, turn-of-the-century Irish playwright, and calls for your careful attention, as follows:

> *"The reasonable person adapts himself to the world; the unreasonable person persists to adapt the world to himself. Therefore all progress depends on the unreasonable person."*

Clear enough, wouldn't you agree? This means that if you want to make sure you don't end up succeeding accidentally, you must take the path of being reasonable. To be "reasonable" typically means that you can be talked into or out of almost any position.

To be reasonable means that you can readily accept excuses and explanations for others' shortfalls. It means accepting the world as it is, not requiring that it be what it should be, whether their point of view or yours. It means accepting the proposition that people are *victims* of the way the world works, or of whatever happens. And that your sympathies are with the victims, never with those who achieve no matter the adversity. Appreciate the victims, and be one of them. That way you will be on track to fail, as they are.

> The unreasonable person, by contrast, never waivers, **refusing to let the world or any of the people in it get in the way.** Gandhi was unreasonable. Marie Curie was unreasonable. As were Napoleon, Columbus, and Winston Churchill. And Queen Elizabeth and Alexander the Great. And Shackleton and Thomas Edison.

The nineteenth-century suffragist Elizabeth Cady Stanton, wrote,

"The true woman is as yet a dream of the future."

How more unreasonable can you get than forcing your dream upon the world?

Every scientist who has changed the course of history (Einstein?), every artist who has changed the future of art (Matisse?), every entrepreneur who has changed the history of business (Mary Kay?), every religious leader who has changed the way we live in this world (Juana Ines de la Cruz?), every thinker who has changed the way we think (from Socrates to Virginia Woolf) has been "unreasonable." That's what you must, with all of the powers you can muster, *AVOID*.

To fail on purpose, you need to be reasonable. You need to be infinitely adaptable. You need to be one with the clichés of the day – people or ideas. You need to be agreeable – to let your destiny be in the direction everyone seems to be going, but getting there faster and on purpose. You need to get along with everyone. To be liked. To play the game. The path to failure is to be increasingly irrelevant to the course of history, and therefore to yourself. In the land of the failed, irrelevance is king.

Here's a brief exchange. Assume that the first one to speak is you – or someone you know. Assume the other voice is that of a guru of how to fail.

"Does this mean that if I am unreasonable I will achieve great things?"

"Absolutely not! But it does mean that if you have a compelling aim in life, you won't achieve it unless you can, when it's called for, be 'unreasonable.' "

> *"So what must I do to avoid the possibility of succeeding in that way?"*
>
> "In all things, adapt yourself to whatever is going on, and to whatever persons are present."
>
> *"But suppose I disagree?"*
>
> "Don't. Unless you do so in the most politic manner."
>
> *"That sounds easy enough."*
>
> "It should. It's the way most people perform socially. And it is by far the easiest path to take in life."
>
> *"Path? To where?"*
>
> "To mediocrity or less (to failure by default). So you'll have to make considerable effort to fail on purpose. Do you think what you've asked is 'unreasonable'?"
>
> *"No."*
>
> "Well, there you have it. You can literally 'fall into' what you have to do. You just have to do it better than others."

That's full of lessons, isn't it? For example, if you hang out with people who are always "reasonable," you will not be pushed out of your comfort zone, and thus you will fail. Or, if you're just like everyone else, you will fail the way they do. Most people don't know how to be unreasonable with themselves; adore yourself as you are. But you have to be ever vigilant to avoid succeeding by default.

Second Lesson:

Hang out with other reasonable people.

By now you know you won't get much credit for succeeding by default. What makes you think you could fail by default and still get credit for failing on purpose?

In his book, *The Angel's Dictionary* (a take-off on Ambrose Bierce's *The Devil's Dictionary*), Edmund Volkart tells us that ***Reason*** is

> *"An excuse, offered as an explanation."*

What a wonderful world you will inhabit, where you will not achieve anything but a superior level of excuse-mongering, much appreciated by your even-more-reasonable apprentices.

Is it reasonable to expect projects to meet deadline and stay on budget? Not for the reasonable person – who has learnt all sorts of excuses and explanations. Is it reasonable to own up to errors and mistakes? It is not, of course, unless you make the error of being unreasonable.

Expecting excellence is unreasonable. Stick with the reasonable approach. It's your ticket to exemplary failure.

A failure's heaven: where the only competition is that of determining who is the cleverest at inventing excuses for failures to perform as intended. There are evangelists for this way of life in every mediocre organization. **You must strive to be the best who has ever lived at being tolerant of everyone and everything** – of having at the ready or accepting from others any plausible excuse for failing to accomplish what needed to be accomplished.

Being "reasonable" is a sort of "Don't rock my boat and I won't rock yours" way of life.

It's one good way we have of helping each other to fail. Become an expert at this. Don't say what you mean. Say what you think the other person wants to hear.

Don't be a "rate-buster" and actually stand out at work as an accomplisher. Develop a perfunctory smile, and agree with what anyone else says. Say only what others will agree with.

Don't be a trouble-maker; someone might think you have real potential.

Play the game that losers play. Just play it better than they do. Be a consummate politician.

Always be "reasonable."

You know what you're aiming for – failing on purpose. Just do it.

Recipe #10

How to Fake Other People Out

"Faking it," as you know, is a technique for avoiding an unpleasant confrontation. It's a way of trying to create a reality that transports you out of a sequence of events in real life – events you want to avoid or escape from. Deceiving others in order to avoid a distasteful reality is, as you know, standard practice in social and in organizational life.

People tell each other what they imagine will avoid undesirable consequences for them. The "truth" becomes the victim. But better the "truth" be the victim than one of us, right?

"Lying" is, as you know, one of the fundamental social graces. Young children are trained in lying as early as possible. They know early on that their parents lie to them, that their friends lie to them, that the media lie to them. So they do what they have learned how to do from observing everyone around them doing it. They lie back. By the time they are verbal, they have become proficient in this social skill.

First Lesson:

Lying is one of the fundamental social graces.

Here's Dorothy Parker's take on how this works in important things, like love and marriage:

"By the time you say you're his,
Shivering and sighing
And he vows his passion is
Infinite, undying –
Lady, make a note of this:
One of you is lying."

She could have been talking about what goes on in organizations. She could have been talking about you and your closest associates. It's often like a masked ball, isn't it?

People tell other people what they think those other people want to hear. It could be flattery, but more often than not it is manipulative. Or they say or do what they think might benefit them in some way, hoping to make others think better of them – or to avoid certain consequences they imagine might be unpleasant or difficult.

When a colleague says, "Let me be truthful about this," it makes you suspicious, doesn't it? **The "truth" of the matter depends upon what you consider to be the truth, not what the other person considers to be the truth.** If they come together, fine. But if not, that other person couldn't be telling you the truth, right? Little wonder people tell us what they think we want to hear – it's the only "truth" we are open to.

The social world moves on pretense, bluffing, kowtowing, in duplicity, hypocrisy, and deceit. If you were to tell someone else the "truth," that person wouldn't believe you if it was not, to that person, something he or she already believed. So you play the game.

And that's why very few people are into art. Here's the tip from Picasso:

"Art is a lie that enables us to realize the truth."

Most people live in a world of the deceptions and posturing produced by other people, and have no interest in realizing any truth that might be revealed there. We have to move forward, not sideways. And we have to move forward on what people say and do, which is the only "truth" we have to go on. If someone tells you a lie in order to get you to see "the truth," is that deception? If someone tells you a lie in order to deceive you, is that the same thing? Do we *realize* the truth, or do we create it?

Two things are of key importance to you here:

- One is that people do indeed *succeed* by lies and deceit. So you're more likely to fail by telling the truth (if you can figure out what *that* is) than you are by being even a mediocre liar/hypocrite.
- The other is that if you are going to play the game that others play, you simply have to be better at it than they are.

Let's see how Lyle did it:

> *Lyle had been so good at faking it over so many years that he had lost himself in the process. No one could detect a real person behind his masks. He was so hopelessly addicted to bluffing his way through everything that he no longer knew how to do anything but 'fake' it. He was like a "shape-shifter," changing persona and style and point of view depending on who was around. He was ostensibly an executive. A fake, but a good one.*
>
> *We do what we get good at, and we get good at what we do.*
>
> *Lyle was an impeccable dresser. He was articulate, always smiling, and very polite.*

> *He asked people's opinions about everything, and then took their opinions as his own.*
>
> *So he was well liked.*
>
> *He couldn't "read" people, because he assumed that, like him, there was nothing there beyond the surface. Unfortunately, he couldn't read the financials either. He simply asked other people for their interpretations, and then took those as his own.*
>
> *Sometimes he wondered, looking into his own smoking mirrors, who he was. But a glance at his paycheck revealed the answer. It had his name on it. And that was good enough evidence for him.*
>
> *Eventually, people tired of his vapidity. Someone said that talking to him was like "punching air." So, he was put out to pasture in his early fifties, far too late to save the company. But somewhat early for someone who hadn't had a thought of his own for forty years.*
>
> *Still, he was good at what he did – faking it.*
>
> *It was reported that he was not able to fake his death.*

As Abraham Lincoln put it:

> ***"It is true that you may fool all the people some of the time; you can even fool some of the people all the time; but you can't fool all of the people all the time."***

But you can be one of those people who keep trying. It'll help you achieve what you want to achieve – your notable failure.

The more time and effort you put into faking other people out, the less time and effort you will have available for actually being successful. The more you succeed in faking yourself and other people out, the more successful you will be at failing in the real world. Unless, of course, this is central to the culture of your organization, in which case you could succeed by default. So you simply have to be world-class at faking it, a star among all the amateurs.

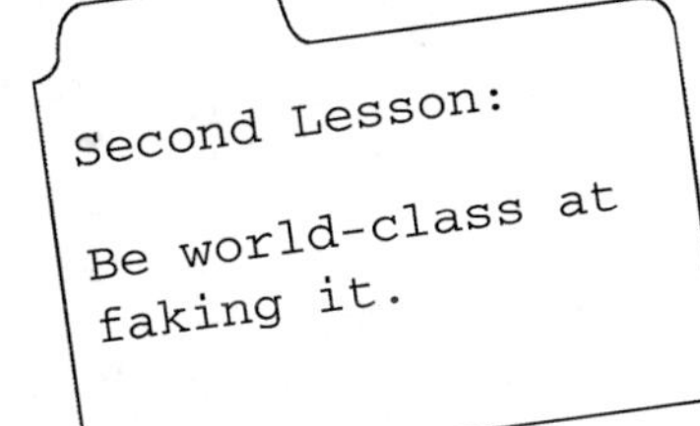

We all tell stories. And we almost always spin those stories to our advantage. Go just a little further. Spin your stories so that they are to the *disadvantage* of others. When they catch on, they'll be not-so-silent conspirators in your decline and fall. If you consistently hire people who will be your shills in your fakery, they will also speed you on your way to your failure. Surround yourself with people who encourage you and make you a better faker.

Fortunately for your cause, there is always a significant danger in self-deception. Especially when you credit yourself with capabilities you believe you have because you have heard other people credit you with those capabilities. This makes the point:

> *As we all know, Harry Houdini exposed himself to many rigorous physical challenges. One day in 1926, an amateur boxer asked Houdini if he could really withstand heavy blows to his midsection as he had publicly claimed. Houdini said of course he could. Whereupon the boxer landed three blows to Houdini's abdomen. Within a day he was feverish – he died within a week of a ruptured appendix and peritonitis.*

People who do not know what they claim to know, or are not capable of what they claim to be capable, usually meet a situation that takes them down. Even magicians. So you are on the right road when you do those things. **Fake yourself and other people into believing that you are somebody you are not.** Sooner better than later, you'll crash and burn.

The historian Barbara Tuchman says that wooden-headedness is the source of self-deception. This becomes a matter of trying to fake out reality. People are easy. They are faking it just like you are. But reality ultimately can't be faked out. To fail with panache, always assume that you're the one who could do it.

Bill Cosby once quipped,

"I don't know the key to success. But the key to failure is trying to please everybody."

Try it. It'll work for you.

***If* you can make it obvious.**

Recipe #11

How to Fill Your Days with Unimportant Things

It may not be the fastest way – or the most dramatic, but the surest path to failure is to focus your attention as exclusively as you can on unimportant things. Do this over a few years and you will get very good at it.

Life, as we all know, consists of what you think about all day. So the less important the things are that you think about all day, the less important you will be. Pay attention to the most trivial, mundane happenings and you are certain to make a mighty contribution to your failure. When you are *event-driven,* as contrasted with *purpose-driven*, you will effortlessly fade away from relevance to others, to your organization, to the rest of the world and, most poignantly, from much – if any – relevance to yourself. The aim is to be meaningless. As you focus on the less-than-meaningful events of the day, you will be gathering impetus for the path you need to be on – the path to failure by choice.

First Lesson:

Focus on the less meaningful events of the day.

If you are not in the throes of a cause that is more important to you than you are, it will seem natural to be event-driven, to be pushed and pulled hither and thither by the trivial events of the day. In fact, this will help you to be *unable* to discriminate what's important from what's not. When you cross that threshold, you've got it made.

Does this help?

> *When all events are equally important, then no event is important.*

If you let things get your attention in the order they happened, then nothing will seem more important than anything else. If all things are equally important, they become unimportant. The more unimportant are the things you deal with, the less important you will be. Way to go.

Bernard Levin, in the quote below, was writing about bureaucrats (but thinking and doing like a "bureaucrat" is the right road for you):

> *"The persistence of public officials [bureaucrats] varies inversely with the importance of the matter on which they are persisting."*

Work on it until you are world-class in persisting at matters which are less and less important. You will lose your way and take everyone else with you. But it's a great strategy for your purposes.

Take care here. The more unimportant the matter on which you are persisting, the more likely you are to be successful, but only in a *bureaucratic* organization. Notice where you are. Champion the important things in a truly bureaucratic organization, and you will be pressured out. You fail one way in an effective organization, just the opposite way in a bureaucratic one. Another paradox to challenge you in your mission to fail successfully.

Merely drifting into failure alongside the large numbers of other drifters failing by default won't do. You have to **cleverly avoid what is important, and practice filling your days with the flotsam of the day.** If you don't know how to do this, observe carefully those who do. Now – understand that you don't want to *be* like them. You want to outdo them, so that others will notice how totally superior you are in the relentless pursuit of unimportant things.

Master the methods for wasting your time and your life on unimportant things. Arrive at mediocrity or even more notable failure before the hordes get there. Missing an important meeting because you were counting your paperclips will help you on your way. So will droning on in a meaningless meeting.

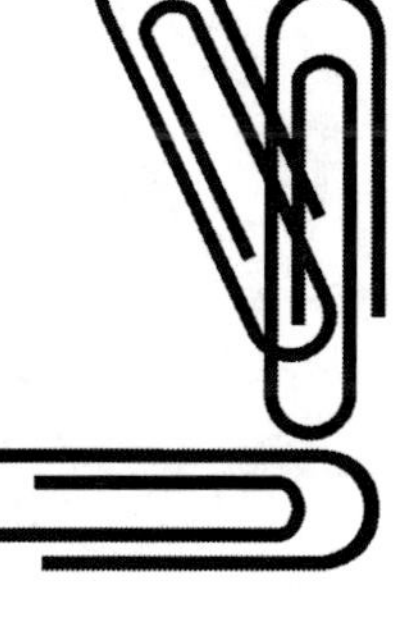

Think about and measure yourself by this:

> *The more time you devote to unimportant things, the more impotent you become as an executive and as a human being.*

There is no pill for curing this condition. It's just the slipperiest of the slippery slopes. Let's tune into this stimulatingly mediocre conversation between George and Vic:

> *George and Vic were having a cool one while waiting for their lunch.*
>
> George: *"How's it going, Vic?"*
>
> Vic: *"Okay, I guess. You know, same-o, same-o."*
>
> George: *"Seems like a lot going on. New CEO. Looks like she'll be making some changes. And the new ERP system, some real challenges there."*

Vic: *"Yeah, I suppose. I'm not much of a computer guy myself."*

George: *"Well, I notice you're never without your 'planner.' Must be really busy."*

Vic: *"Oh, yeah! Look at this. I've got wall-to-wall meetings."*

George: *"Must be hard to keep up."*

Vic: *"Yeah, it is. Seems like I just keep falling behind. We were supposed to evaluate the impact of the new ERP system three months ago. I haven't gotten around to it yet."*

George: *"What d'ya think of the new CEO?"*

Vic: *"She's okay, I guess. I haven't actually met her. I was supposed to meet with her shortly after she came on board – what was that, two, three months ago? Just been too busy.*

George: *"What's on for this afternoon?"*

Vic: *"Well, something came up this morning about an audit we did last year. Gotta get to the bottom of that. Then I've gotta meet with Jim. He's having some problems at home."*

Their lunch came.

And it was time to move on to important things. Like Vic's forthcoming dental appointment.

Well, you've been there, done that. The best candidates for failure become masterful at attributing to themselves a level of importance that far exceeds any reality. For the failure-in-progress, what *is* important is himself and his busywork. You need to be able to figure out how to *appear* to be the most important cog in the machine, the busiest person around – as long as there is no measure of real accomplishment. This is a tough challenge. Many others will be competing for the limelight. Perform your over-whelming busyness and thus your self-importance, openly and with flair. People will be glad to help you fail just to get rid of you – you and your challenge to *their* self-importance.

Second Lesson:

Appear to be busy with important but irrelevant matters.

As is often said,

> *"The devil is in the details."*

On the other hand, we are often told,

> *"Don't sweat the small stuff."*

What's a pointless person to do?

It isn't the size of things that matters. It is their importance or relevance to a cause, or a mission. Thus importance or relevance can only be ascertained relative to some over-arching cause or mission. Just don't have one. That way almost everything you settle your attention on can be unimportant.

The more you use yourself exclusively as the measure of the importance of things, the more certain of failure you can be. The more unimportant the things you pay attention to all day, the less relevant you will be to yourself and your organization.

> *If you're full of yourself, you can easily fill your day with unimportant things, beginning with yourself.*

Exhibit and promote your accomplishments as a pointless person. The reason?

> *The unimportant person seeks to appear to BE important. The person who will succeed seeks to DO the important.*

Clear enough if you want to fail. Appear to BE important. Don't DO important.

It helps, of course, if you can daily lose some capability for determining what's important and what is not. The way to do that is to cease to care. Be indifferent. Be "democratic" – treat all information that comes your way as equal. Scoff at what other people consider to be important. (Or at other people who think they're more important!)

There was once a guy who thought that "Anonymous" was the name of the person who was responsible for what was written. Don't DO anonymous. BE anonymous. Stand out in the crowd by fitting in. Be the voice of the irrelevant. Have no apparent cause in life. But pursue it diligently and creatively.

When it becomes more important for you to appear to *be* important than to *do* anything really important, you've crossed a key threshold in your campaign.

Recipe #12

How to Be Indecisive

Let's see, how *would* one decide how to introduce a subject like this one – how to be indecisive? Well, maybe we shouldn't have started that way, but ... Is it possible that thinking about it as follows would help?

"When all candles be out, all cats are gray."

You can have all sorts of excitation trying to decide what *that* means. Some really smart folk reckon it means that the less light you can bring to bear on what you are observing or being told, the more things look alike. Reality fades to shades of gray for people who do not have their own headlights on high beam. So they often cannot figure out what's what. They expect (or hope for?) "reality" to push them in the right direction. But they don't have the mental horsepower to discern and decide. They are making a decision in the dark, which is risky and uncertain.

So the more you keep yourself in deep twilight by having no lights of your own to illuminate the world around you, the greater your contribution will be to your intended failure.

First Lesson:

Keep yourself in the dark.

So far it sounds easy. Stupid people often wonder what's going on. That's because they can't shine the right kind of light (from themselves) on the world. It's as if they intended to be victimized by their own shortfalls. It is certainly the case that smart people fail. But they fail by being temporarily stupid. There's where you want your failure-bent mentality to take over.

Isn't it remarkable how, when you put a group of people in a "meeting," the level of indecisiveness goes up a notch or two? And the level of any consequential responsibility goes down. People can even be animated in boring meetings – but only when they themselves are holding forth. But by the time the meeting is over and they amble back in the direction of their offices or work stations, it's back to business-as-usual. Is that because those people don't have their own lights on, and therefore all of the talk that goes on appears to everyone as being "gray" – sort of indistinguishable from most of the other meetings they have attended?

Never quite going anywhere but to the next meeting about much the same kinds of issues. But then petty people have to nourish and perpetuate their petty concerns, don't they? Business-as-usual has a heavy-duty motive behind it, more potent than most managers are.

IF you distribute the task of making intelligent decisions to as many people as you can involve, *and* ... IF you make sure those people don't have enough candle-power to really illuminate the task, **THEN ... you can be certain that the outcome of your collective deliberations will be wheel-spinning.**

"Deliberation: The act of examining one's bread to determine which side it is buttered on."

(from Bierce's *The Devil's Dictionary*)

People who are themselves indecisive will both call and attend more meetings. But no committee was ever awarded a Nobel Prize for an intellectual breakthrough.

However, there lurks a paradox here in certain (conventional) organizations. It was well set forth by Sir Thomas Brewbold, quoted in Bierce's dictionary:

"For whereas there is but one way to do nothing and diverse ways to do something, but only one is the right way, it follows that he who from indecision stands still has not so many chances of going astray as he who pushes forward."

In other words, the decisive person could be wrong. The indecisive person may be favored in certain organizations simply because he or she makes fewer mistakes. That's the way bureaucrats get ahead. Since you do not want to get ahead but be turned out sooner rather than later into the pasture crowded with other failures, the lesson is clear: you must appear to be decisive about inconsequential things, but let other fools take the rap for making decisions about important things that could turn out to be wrong.

But whoever said failing on purpose was easy?

Here's a short story worth reflecting on:

During the Civil War, the North's General Ulysses S. Grant was conferring with General Gordon Granger about Granger's notable success in a combat situation.

"Your prompt decision to attack," Grant said, "was admirable. You had but five minutes to decide."

"Yes, sir," the victorious Granger replied, "it is a great thing to know exactly what to do

> *in an emergency. When in doubt whether to attack or retreat I never hesitate a moment – I toss up a copper."*
>
> *"Do you mean to say," Grant replied incredulously, "that's what you did this time?"*
>
> *"Yes, General, I did. But for Heaven's sake, don't reprimand me. I disobeyed the coin."*

Think about that. To fail on purpose means you have to *avoid* getting lucky.

Finesse yourself away from tough or controversial issues. Keep a low profile. Avoid conflict. Play politics. In most organizations, it's better to play politics than it is to make a bad decision. In many (conventional) organizations, you may actually be rewarded for failing to do your job. So the trick is how to fail in your role without being rewarded for doing so. And the technique is to be so indecisive that it drives even mediocre people to want you gone. They want a decision to be made. They just don't want to be the one making it. Be the master of indecisiveness.

Don't champion a bad decision – or a good one. Since you can't know for sure whether it's a good one or a bad one beforehand, the best course of action is to avoid taking a stand until all the dust has settled. *Then* take a position and you can always be "right." This will irritate even the most competent people, who will join the losers in getting rid of you.

As British Prime Minister Bevan put it more than a half-century ago,

> *"We all know what happens to people who stay in the middle of the road. They get run over."*

Be *there.* Perhaps this expresses it better. The eighteenth-century English cleric and wine-merchant(!) Charles Colton advised,

> *"Deliberate with caution, act with decision and promptness."*

Do it the other way around: Deliberate without caution. Then act indecisively, and always with bad timing.

And always remember the words of Peter Alliss, who wrapped it up in a ribbon for us:

> *"He used to be indecisive, but now he's not so certain."*

Or those of Oscar Levant:

> *"Once I make up my mind, I'm full of indecision."*

Let that be said of you.

What attracts lemmings (even though it is more myth than fact) is that the lead lemmings always go over the cliff decisively. People don't care so much if their leaders are wrong, as long as they are decisive. To avoid having followers – who might inadvertently make you successful in spite of your commitment to the opposite path – be indecisive, and helplessly so, when they are looking to you to be decisive. Be deliberate but pompous in your indecisiveness.

Since most people don't know, or care, where they're going in life, you have to be careful that your purpose (to fail on purpose) isn't apparent to others. They need to see your indecisiveness as a character flaw, not as a technique. Then you will seem to be like them, only more deserving of understanding. It is, after all, not your fault that you are indecisive. Let your case be hopeless, but "tragic."

Get stymied by the most trivial decisions. But come down on the big ones without giving them a thought. That way you can contribute to your failure both ways. People will attribute your poor decisions to your indecisiveness. Cunning.

No matter your decisions, always express doubt that they were the right ones. Especially if they turn out well, express your belief that they were faulty. Make it a practice to critique what others consider a good decision, and to praise what others believe to be a poor decision. That will make it appear that you don't know the good from the bad, and thus add to your reputation as being indecisive.

We could stop here, but that would require a decision. What do *you* think?

Recipe #13

How to Be Able Not to Think

You would think, wouldn't you, that most people don't need much counsel on the matter of not being able to think. Still, notable competence at anything – including failing on purpose – requires some exceptional effort in developing the habits needed to carry you to your goal.

Of course, the best way to equip oneself to be unable to think would be that of never having engaged in it in any serious way in the past. It's obvious that this technique works for most people. But, you may be setting out with a handicap here.

Do not fall into despair. Like any other habit, once your autopilot gets the hang of not thinking, you'll be able not to think all day long. In fact, you'll become addicted to the ease and the self-indulgent rewards that accrue to people who become constitutionally incapable of thinking. This disability is a condition that will greatly facilitate your social life, as you have undoubtedly noticed in others who are more afflicted than you are.

If yours is a large organization, and quite bureaucratic, developing habits to become proficient at not thinking will also contribute greatly to your rise in the organization. After all, men have been elected to the highest office in the land because they were less able to think than their opponent. It's a condition that appeals to voters and to subordinates – this inability to think. Keep in mind that people prefer other people in charge who are more like them. Surely, if not thinking works for them, it will work for you!

```
First Lesson:

Be less capable
of thinking than
anyone around you.
```

If you are going to use this stratagem to facilitate your failure as an executive, you have to be less capable of thinking than anyone around you – up, down, left, right or in any other direction. This is going to take diligence on your part, and lots of practice. The way you ordinarily walk or talk is just a bundle of habits, from fixing your morning coffee to brushing your teeth at night. Not being able to think has to become a superlative, well-honed, set of virtuoso habits you must achieve and exercise.

Most people can get reasonably good at it simply by not thinking about it. But you must be better than others. Obviously you can't always be thinking about how not to think. You have to, almost unthinkingly, identify and emulate the best role models that have ever existed. If you are already world-class at not being able to think, try using a mirror for your role model. Or an audio or video tape; seeing and hearing yourself not thinking can provide you with endless examples to emulate. Then you can perfect your performance.

Another option is to go to the history books. There are many exemplars. Remember this from Bertrand Russell, the philosopher?

> *"Many people would sooner die than think."*

That is not idle chatter. Take note, they *do*.

Here, for example, are Shirley and Barb:

> *Shirley is talking to her friend Barb about her new-found cause in life:*
>
> Shirley: *"Barb, I've decided I want to fail on purpose – not just by default like most of the people I know. And I know you're kind of an expert in this – you know, three or four failed marriages, your inability to keep a job for more than six months, the fact that you're just drifting through life, and ..."*
>
> Barb: *"Hey, I could take that as a criticism, you know."*
>
> Shirley: *"Well, I meant it as a kind of compliment. You're experienced in these things. You seem happier now just because you don't much give a hang about things, anymore. I want you to be my coach. I'm tired of striving only to be stepped on one more time. But it seems stupid to just fail by default. There ought to be a way of speeding this along and arriving in this world of yours where you don't have to give a hang anymore."*
>
> Barb: *"Well, I'll tell you what one of my therapists told me. She said that not being able to think is one of the keys. And that it is trickier than most people imagine because, as*

she said, thinking is like a muscle. It has to be developed. If it's not exercised for a period of time, it decays and dies. So I figure there are two ways of having an advantage over others here. One is to be born to parents and a social network that does not encourage you to be a thinker in the first place. But if it's too late for that (I don't think it is in your case), then it's pretty clear that hanging out with other people who are incapable of thinking – you know, like many of our own managers – will snuff out whatever flickerings of being able to think you had in the first place."

Shirley: *"Wow! It seems so easy."*

Barb: *"It isn't. Look how long it took me to get to where I am. I had a boss one time who told me I had a real talent – for being unable to think. I guess there are some people who are pretty good at detecting this. Myself, I can't figure out other people who just can't do it."*

Shirley: *"Well, as they say, 'Birds of a feather flock together.' At least we can swing the vote."*

You think that's not believable? How do you think people *do* become mediocre (or less) in droves? They didn't figure out how to do this all by themselves. They learned it. Maybe you're not talking to the people who have really succeeded at being *unable* to think. They're the people you need to hang out with. Think about that before it is too late. Maybe you're already surrounded by people who can't think. If so, you've got a leg up on this thing.

Assuming that you were one of the few who was equipped to think at birth, this disability can be overcome. You have the ultimate weapon to guarantee your inability to think. That weapon is **simply not exercising your mind muscles until they finally atrophy.** Your thinking abilities will eventually fade away and you will actually be incapable of thinking.

Often attributed to Einstein, but also to Henry Ford, this quote may help you grasp the importance of what we're talking about,

> *"Thinking is hard work. That's why so few do it."*

H. L. Mencken, known for his caustic wit, reckoned,

> *"... well over 80% of the human race goes through life without a single original thought."*

Go with this huge majority. Join the ranks of the unthinking. Be "empowered" by them.

Second Lesson:

Be empowered by the unthinking.

Lest you still believe there is not an incidental advantage to this business of not being able to think, look at what James Thurber, widely known for his cutting observations, had to say about it:

> *"Sixty minutes of thinking of any kind is bound to lead to confusion and unhappiness."*

Maybe that's why Barb seemed to be so happy in her circumstances?

Add to that the fact that people who are incapable of thinking often *agree* with each other (as Thomas Paine observed back in the eighteenth-century) far more than do people who are forever thinking about things.

And if you are achieve this level of being able not to think, it may help to know that you may be contributing significantly to the health of the larger society. According to Lucas Cleeve:

> *"For God's sake, don't let us think. If we did there would be an end to society."*

The more able you are to be unable to think, **the more you will contribute to your own cause – to fail on purpose – and the more you will contribute to the failure of your organization and the failure of the larger society.** A three-fer: while achieving your own failure, you can contribute a bit to the failure of your organization and of the larger society at the same time.

Need some thought-prodders?

- Telling people what you know is not thinking. Don't think about what the problem actually requires. Just tell people what you know (mostly from other people).
- Telling people what *you* assume *they* ought to know is not thinking. "Them who can't DO, teach." This is a form of pontificating.
- Telling yourself what you already know is not thinking. Talking to yourself may be a good way of avoiding becoming smarter and capable of thinking. Do lots of that.
- Being open to all kinds of things you have no need to know is not thinking. People who have no aim in life have an infinite capacity for irrelevancies. Master the technique of being the passive receiver of…whatever.
- Always have "the" answer. Requires no thinking. Getting stuck because you don't know the answer might require you to start thinking. Don't do that!

You get the point. Don't fall into the trap of thinking. It could get to be a habit. And that would take you off course, and thus destroy your chosen legacy to the world.

The good news is that you can do this almost without thinking. Let the flotsam and the jetsam of the world's unthinkers wash over you until you become as useless as their blather. Expose yourself at every opportunity to thoughtlessness and you will become capable of producing it – without even thinking about it.

Recipe #14

How to Avoid Being Accountable

It may be eye-opening to reflect on the fact that "accountability" varies inversely with your position in the organization.

The people who do the real work of the organization are the ones who are held most accountable. That is because it is easier to count hours and material than it is to count performance.

The closer you get to the "top" of the typical hierarchical organization, the less accountability there is. It is assumed to be difficult or impossible to measure the performance of managers and executives. In any conventional organization, the least "accountable" person is usually the CEO or the President. Especially if he or she owns the place.

To whom is the chief executive "accountable"? In the typical organization, to no one other than himself or herself. The assumption being, apparently, that by reaching the top, this person has enough self-discipline to be self-accountable. But that's rarely the case. The top person comes and goes at his or her pleasure, making schedules that are suitable not to a customer, not to a boss, not to the priorities of the company, but to oneself. *Is it possible that this is one reason why so many fail?* May be a clue here. But, you're practicing how not to think, so ...

Add this to your list of the advantageous perversities of life in organizations ("advantageous" because you can take advantage of them for your own cause):

> *The less accountable individuals are, the more passion they seem to be able to muster for attempting to hold **other people** accountable.*

First Lesson:

Be rabid about holding others accountable.

The lesson here is simple enough: Be rabid about wanting to hold other people accountable. Given the formula above, most people will then notice that you do not hold yourself accountable. This is a great and useful recipe for failure.

Times change, skirt lengths go up or down, the world hangs on the activity of one celebrity or another, while the corporate world plays games to determine accountability. "Accountability" is the new buzzword for what used to be known as "responsibility."

Before management became an industry, it was widely believed that people were more or less responsible for the consequences of their actions, or inactions. That's before there was a cadre of white-collar folks to "manage" others. Back in those days, there was the understanding that responsibility was largely *self*-responsibility.

So, if you substitute the term "accountable" for "responsible" in the following, you can see that Evan Esar, American humorist, was up to something insightful:

"If you could kick the person responsible for most of your troubles, you wouldn't be able to sit down for months."

Therefore, if you intend to fail heroically, make sure that others can easily observe you ...

- Espousing your principles and your aims, but never holding yourself accountable for either undertaking them, or fulfilling them.
- Talking incessantly about the need to hold everyone else accountable.
- Blaming others or the circumstances for your own shortfalls.

The social "Darwinist" Herbert Spencer wrote,

"The ultimate result of shielding men from the effects of folly is to fill the world with fools."

You need to complain loudly about other people's incompetence and shortfalls so that, by shielding yourself from your own and actually doing nothing but complaining about theirs, you contribute to filling the organization with fools. **That way you could be the king of fools.**

Let's look in on a CEO, Harry (or it could be Tom or Dick):

Harry, the chief executive, was talking to one of his many consultants about "accountability."

He said, "We've got to do something about making people more accountable around here."

"Well, you know, Harry," the consultant said, "that term is a compound of two words.

> ***Account**, as in taking into account, or actually counting. And the other part of it is **ability**. Can you hold people accountable for something if they don't have the abilities or the competencies to bring that about?"*
>
> *Harry scowls. "You're always screwing with my head," he says. "I don't give a damn whether they are capable or not. They need to be held accountable!"*
>
> *The consultant replied: "If you really believed that Harry, you would hold yourself far more accountable than you do. But I always figured it was because you weren't fully capable yourself of doing everything you're called upon to do that you allowed others to be unaccountable."*

What would be your reaction if someone spoke to you that way? On the other hand, if your customer service people are not capable of performing to the level of their "accountability," knocking the customers' socks off isn't going to happen, no matter how much you holler about … **accountability**.

Second Lesson:

Be vague about your own role.

Edwards Deming wrote that most chief executives don't have a really clear conception of what their job is. This means that the more vague you can be about your role in the organization, the less accountable you will be – to yourself, to others, to a board.

Kind of a psychological form of "dodgem."

Keep in mind that accountability requires visibility and measurability. One way of avoiding accountability is to make your life at work opaque: everyone assumes you are there, but make it difficult for them to get to you. You know, be so superior to them that you no more than occasionally deign to have direct contact with them.

If you're never visible, it's hard to be accountable, isn't it? Mediocre employees (including mediocre managers and executives) have known this for years. Many are past masters at being anonymous and invisible. You can't hold people accountable if you can't find them, or if they're hiding in a crowd. For then you can't be quite sure whose fault it was that the report didn't get written, the orders didn't get filled, or the job didn't get done. Or, done well. These techniques will work for you if you perfect them.

You probably remember Groucho Marx's famous line:

> *"I wouldn't want to belong to any club that would have me as a member."*

There's more here than mere cleverness. One example: most employees secretly understand that any organization that would put up with their sub-par performance is not the kind of organization they would actually want to work for. They're unhappy because they can't respect a company that would have them as employees. As their boss, consider this: employees who don't respect you because you put up with their laziness, indifference, and incompetence are not likely to bust their buns trying to make you successful. With very little effort you, too, can have employees who wouldn't want to belong to an organization that would have them as members.

You have the trump card. In any gathering, if you're the one with the most power, you will be the least accountable. Power and accountability are inversely related. **To avoid being accountable, always be the one with the most power.** Who's going to be courageous (or foolish) enough to try to bell *that* cat?

Be quick to take credit for anything good that happens. And be equally quick to blame someone (or something) else for anything bad that happens. **Over time, you will create a mythology of "non-accountability" that works well in most organizations. And, over time, no one will believe you either way.** When that happens, you will have created a way of avoiding accountability. When people can't take you seriously, you will then be outside the *realm* of accountability.

Being irrelevant may be the best way of avoiding the accountability. Be the most irrelevant executive in the executive suite – and you'll be moving on to spectacular failure. It's your right. Exercise it!

Recipe #15

How to Grow and Enhance Bad Habits

People do not "have" habits. Habits "have" people. People do not *use* habits. They are used by them. Your habits determine who you are, where you're going, and how you are going to get there. In a contest between habits and will, always bet on habits. You may want to achieve certain things. But no amount of desire or "motivation" will make this happen. Your habits will either take you there, or to some other destination.

You may desire to be successful. But you won't be unless you have the habits necessary to get you there. You may decide you want to fail by design, by intention. But you can't do this either unless you have the kinds of habits that will take you there.

Habits behave us. We don't behave them. We are who we are because we have the kinds of habits we have. There is no psychological folderol – e.g., "motivation" – that can overcome habits. People who are competent have the kinds of habits that make it *necessary* for them to be competent. People who are incompetent have the kinds of habits that make it *necessary* for them to be incompetent. Neither condition can be chosen in the short term. They both depend on growing and enhancing the kinds of habits that make one or the other condition a necessary one for you.

We might rephrase an old saying thus:

> *First we make our habits, and then our habits make us.*

You can't fail magisterially (or well before others dawdle into that state late in life) unless you seed and feed the kinds of habits that will make it inevitable. You can't fail just because you "want" to. You've got to have the right kinds of habits to make that happen in spite of chance events that might take you off in the opposite direction.

First Lesson:

Seed and feed the habits that make failure inevitable.

As Dostoevski, the renowned Russian writer, once commented,

> *"The second half of a man's life is made up of nothing but the habits acquired during the first half."*

The "second half" seems to start earlier and earlier. It now begins, it seems, around 10-11 years of age, when most young folk begin to assume that no one knows as much as they do. Or when they begin, at any age, to assume the world began the day they were born. Now there's a "bad" habit you can, with practice, develop into one of your trademarks.

Consider Samuel Johnson's brief observation:

> *"The chains of habit are too weak to be felt until they are too strong to be broken."*

Ah! ..."the chains" of habit. By the time you're aware of them, it is too late to escape their hold over you.

They are all-powerful and indispensable accomplices in your mission to fail before others do, and to do so with verve and flair. Get your habits aligned to your mission of failing on purpose, and you will have optimized the likelihood of fulfilling it.

People talk loosely about "good" habits and "bad" habits. Presumably they can be identified in one camp or the other independently of the context. You must disagree. You must be more outcome-oriented. For our purposes, a "good" habit is one that is supposed to lead to your success in life. And a "bad" habit is therefore one that propels you in the opposite direction. Thus the necessity to talk about making and enhancing bad habits. "Good," for your purposes.

All habits are but means to an end. They're good if they get you to where you want to go, bad if they don't. **So certain habits others consider bad will be good for your purposes.** Since most people assume that good habits will make you successful, you simply want to nourish those habits that will contribute notably to your failure.

In the following conversation, Adam is the one who is trying to program himself for failure, although he isn't aware of it, whereas Seth is trying to program himself for success, even though he lands on a different idea everyday. Why they are talking to each other is anyone's guess.

> Seth: *"Adam, I was reading just the other day that what we so casually refer to as the 'culture' of this organization is really no more than the operative habits of the people who work here over time. What do you think of that idea?*
>
> Adam: *"Well, I never thought about it. And I'm not much of a reader. Seems like a waste of time to me. It seems to me you either like a place or you don't. People seem to manage to fail whether it's a good organization or a bad one."*

Seth: *"Well, it just seemed like a way of accounting for why the culture of a place like this is the way it is. You don't agree?*

Adam: *"Well, I'm not disagreeing. I just don't know what you could do with an idea like that. I don't see what habits have to do with it. They don't affect me much one way or the other. I just try to salute the brass, you know. I jump, but never too high or too far. You know, like playing it cool."*

Seth: *"So you're not trying to get ahead?"*

Adam: *"Hell, there ain't no 'ahead.' You're either 'in' or you're 'out.' I've been knowing that for years. What's your problem, and why are you doing all that reading? Is that going to get you 'ahead'? You think talking smart is going to grease your slide uphill?"*

The way people see things is driven by habit. The way people talk is driven by habit. The way people think or feel is driven by habit. Do you, for example, choose your habits or merely accept them as a part of who you "are"? If you can't make them work for you, then you will be working for them. This must be the original "squirrel cage."

What are these "bad" habits you need to grow and enhance? And, exactly where do they come from? Bad habits are the ones that helped others to achieve their failure.

To enhance your bad habits you should:

- Study the failures of other executives carefully to determine just what habits enabled them to fail, or disabled them from succeeding.

- Study the underlying habits of those few executives who have been successful, and then diligently grow the opposite kinds of habits.
- If you begin to be recognized as having "the right stuff" for your role, be sure that those who recognize this in you are great candidates for their own failure. Otherwise, get a different cheering section.
- If you turn in a poor performance by accident, seek out the root cause and equip yourself to perform poorly by habit.
- Read all you can from the popular business press about how to be successful. Follow that advice. Apparently, that will help you to fail.
- Surround yourself with marginally-competent people, and heed their advice, their ideas, and their beliefs.
- Slavishly follow every fad that comes your way, until the next one comes along.
- Think in clichés and speak in clichés so you can perform like a cliché.
- Never walk your talk, but talk your walk, whatever that happens to be today.
- Seek balance in your life so your family and friends can be as mistreated by your incompetencies as your peers and your subordinates are.

- Find a "sure-fire" recipe for success, and grow it into a set of habits. They will be "bad" enough to propel you on your way.

Self-help author, Samuel Smiles, [1812-1904] once put it thus:

"Sow a thought, and you reap an act;
Sow an act, and you reap a habit;
Sow a habit, and you reap a character;
Sow a character, and you reap a destiny."

Some people develop the habit of forever trying to change other people's habits, *having despaired of changing their own.*

Don't despair. It will require your full attention to develop and enhance the kinds of habits that will make for your own failure. Let others fail by default. They don't need your help to fail. To fail heroically will be your legacy. Don't share it with those who are ambiguous about failure, but certain to get there by default.

Recipe #16

How to Miscast People – Including Yourself

Most people who are cast in the role of executive – particularly chief executive – are miscast. How can that be? As follows (just *some* examples):

- Mediocre executives produce mediocre – or worse – successors.
- People are cast in that role for all kinds of reasons having nothing to do with their qualifications for the role – e.g., politics, family connections, the least-worst candidate, etc.
- There is typically not much clarity about what that role entails.
- There is typically even less clarity about how performance in that role is going to be measured. Or by whom.
- Most of what you have to learn to perform in that role has to be learned by doing it. And by the time most candidates jump into

or are lured into the role, they are years past being capable of learning. So they do their own "thing" because that's all they know how to do.

- The position confers power. As you know, power and accountability are inversely related. And as we have shown previously in this book, few have the courage to bell the cat that has more power than they have.

And on and on. The cards are stacked against performing well in the CEO's role, even if it's you. This is, of course, to your advantage. The challenge is that most of your peers are going to fail by default, and perhaps the majority of those via the sheer gravity pull of mediocrity. It's going to take some dedicated practice to get there before others do, and with panache – having *achieved* something that the others just *tumbled down* into.

```
First Lesson:

Avoid roles you can
perform successfully
(if such exist).
```

Life is a continuous process of being cast in one role or another. And of being pushed or pulled out of one role or another. If you are serious about succeeding at failing on purpose, you have to make certain you don't get yourself accidentally cast in a role in which you can't help but be "successful." Well, maybe there is no such role. It seems people can manage to fail in any role that comes their way. *You* just have to be better at it.

"Role" is a useful metaphor. Shakespeare wrote his now overwhelmingly famous lines, *"All the world's a stage, and all the men and women merely players,"* many years ago, but they are as valid today as they were then. He meant them in a profound way. The lines refer to the roles we perform more or less well in the stories we imagine we are in. Presumably, great performances by the people cast in those roles make a great story come out the way it is supposed to. The better the story, the more demanding the performance. As a practical matter, this means ~~is~~ that if you intend to achieve something truly worthy, not only do you have to be a great performer in your starring role, but you have to surround yourself with great performers in their *supporting* roles.

If you intend to fail on purpose, you have to have people in those supporting roles who can be complicit in your cause.

Most people have figured out how to do this in marriage, for example. But we also see it in organizations. People who are in a story (in which failure is the outcome) intuitively surround themselves with people who can play the supporting roles in such a way that the outcome becomes inevitable. Probably this was not the outcome they intended (if they thought about it; oh, but – we've already established that they probably weren't thinking). But the way they cast themselves and others in the key roles made it happen anyway. Poor performances seem always to produce poor outcomes. Failure to perform your role with great competence, and failure to surround yourself with people in supporting roles who can't perform their roles competently, is what you want to accomplish.

You are enabled and constrained not by your wishes or your hopes and dreams, but by the roles you get cast into in your life. By-and-large, your life is made up of the roles you get cast in, or fall into, or audition for. Lover or chef, manager or machinist, astronaut or fisherman, executive or bum, it is how you *perform* the roles you get yourself cast into that predict to your destiny. Perform them poorly, with the help of those in supporting roles, and you have got your ticket to failure punched.

Founders often miscast themselves as the CEO. For example:

> *Jack is the founder and now the CEO of his company. It has been reasonably successful, either because of or in spite of him.*
>
> *He didn't really want to "run" a company. He was merely having fun doing what he liked to do at the outset, and that turned into an organization. Some days he didn't even want to get up. Much of what he had to do he hated doing. He often felt like he didn't even want to come into the office. He felt stressed. He found himself wondering whether or not he should be doing something other than "running" his organization.*
>
> *He didn't really trust his subordinates to do things the way he would do them. But he didn't see that he had any viable alternatives. To complicate matters, he and his wife were considering a divorce.*
>
> *In short, he didn't like his life. It was not what he expected or where he wanted to be at his age. He would really prefer being on the golf course.*
>
> *Or sipping some exotic drink with some exotic babe on some exotic tropical isle. His fantasy life turned out to be better than his real one.*

> *Like Charlie Brown, he wondered, "How can I fail when I'm so sincere?"*
>
> *His company was limping along, but he considered his own life a failure.*

The possibilities for being miscast are limitless. Every conversation you have with someone alters the path your life will take – in small and large ways. There is only one way of being rightly cast for failure. Just have no clue what that could be. Otherwise, you might succeed by default.

To paraphrase novelist and essayist Christopher Morley,

> *Every role in life is one in which everyone is initially miscast.*

Get miscast. Be incompetent at the outset. **Be indifferent to learning how to perform your role(s).** If you want to hold your head up, you have to fail on purpose. That's why you have this primer in your hands.

You will always be cast in roles which you are initially incompetent to perform. You can always get by. But that's because you are surrounded by people who are no more competent to perform their roles than you are. That's the path to failure. Stay on it.

But, wait! – you might say. Won't one's "experience" automatically make one more capable? Not necessarily. Stupid people don't seem to learn much from experience. Now there's a lesson that can be very useful.

Neither, apparently, do top executives learn from experience. They seem to fail in their next assignments faster than they did in the previous one. That's because, as the baseball player Vernon Law wrote,

> *"Experience is a hard teacher because she gives the test first, the lesson afterwards."*

And also for this reason: Can the mentality with which you created the problem in the first place be adequate for solving it? Lovers "fall" in love, apparently assuming that such a fall carries with it the competence for bringing it off. As do executives often "fall" and make the same assumption. They would be wrong. A role into which you "fall" does not automatically confer on you (or anyone) the competence for performing it.

To distinguish yourself from commonplace failures, or from the rabble of the merely mediocre, you have to have the kind of blind ego and the level of self-deception that enables you to be miscast for a role for which you are uniquely and remarkable incompetent.

American philosopher Elbert Hubbard wrote,

> *"Life is just one damn thing after another."*

He might have said,

> *Life is just one damn miscasting after another.*

Mary Lou Quinlan quit her job as CEO of N. W. Ayer because her job description as CEO was filled with things she didn't like to do and wasn't good at. She was miscast. She didn't wait to fail. So she quit. Don't do what she did. Hang in there until it's clear to everyone that you have *failed* in your role.

Here is Henry Ford's observation on the subject of "casting":

> *"The question, 'Who ought to be boss?' is like asking 'Who ought to be the tenor in the quartet?' Obviously, the man who can sing tenor."*

Times have changed. That measure is no longer used. Who knows? Maybe you got chosen for the role because you *couldn't* sing tenor. Maybe you were meant to be a dancer.

It's almost impossible to fail if you happen to land in the right role. Get the top role because you want it, not because you are willing to learn how to perform it.

In short, first get yourself miscast. Then you will intuitively miscast the people you surround yourself with. For your purposes, that's the way to go. For those who intend to fail on purpose, you simply have to be more ingenious than others at getting yourself miscast.

Then you can fail. Just be sure people suspect you did this on purpose. Make failing an achievement, not a problem to be suffered. Smile, you don't want people to think you are merely incompetent, but helplessly so. Be proud of your achievement. Strike a blow for having a unique purpose that is consistent with reality.

Recipe #17

How to Put Feelings Ahead of Performance

Around the turn of the last century (c.1875-1925), the finishing touches were put on the "psychologizing" of Western civilization. That's a big and fancy term. All it means is that people began focusing much more on their internal condition and, as a result, became the center of the known universe – at least, of *their* known universe.

Here, the result: "*My* feelings, *my* opinions, *my* beliefs come first. Reality? It's what *I* say it is. I'll tell you where the world begins and ends – with *my* thoughts, with *my* feelings."

Although this shift took place slowly over time, it was a huge shift in orientation. It became the core of thought and social relationships across Western civilization.

There was a time, too long ago for many of you to remember, when there was only "we" and "me." There could be a "me" based on how well one fulfilled one's duty to the "we." You would have had a role in your tribe or clan or "family" or community and your status depended on how well you performed that role. Remember, we talked of role playing in Chapter 16? Well, remembering does require some thinking and since we have recommended that you eliminate those habits, you may take our word for it that role playing was discussed in Chapter 16.

What we're saying here is that there was no "I" as we know it until recently. In fact, it's interesting to note that before the Japanese culture was Westernized, there was no word in Japanese equivalent to our "I." Their use of this term is a very recent and very modern thing. Psychology invented the "I" role, as we know it today. Its partner, "ego," is also a very recent concept. Increasingly, people have been tyrannized not by the larger wholes to which they belong, but by their own egos. "I" talks to "me" and causes all kinds of problems (presumably fixable only by psychologists, who created those problems in the first place).

> *A psychologist, as you know, is a person who goes to a strip bar to observe the audience.*

This is far more background than you asked for. But the upshot is simple enough: If you want to fail, be as "psychological" as you can be. Let your ego dominate you. Assume that people are "psychological," that is, that their behavior is caused by forces they are not aware of, but which you, as a tin-horn psychologist, are aware of. Above all, serve yourself. Your feelings about things come first. Manipulate yourself and others with your feelings.

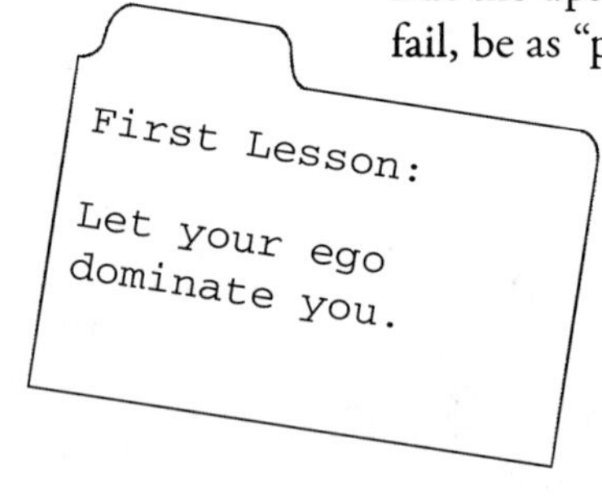

To paraphrase Freud, where "we" were, "I" now is. What this creates is the perpetual adolescent. And what the perpetual adolescent is saying is, "The world (as I know it, of course) has to adapt to ME. What I don't agree with is just plain WRONG. The only thing that really matters is how *I* feel about things."

If you want to fail, it isn't performance that counts; it's feelings. Defer to feelings whenever possible – and sometimes when not possible. Lead with, "I'm not feeling well today," or, "I feel like taking a break," or, "I don't feel like that." Try to manipulate others through their feelings.

It seems widely believed today that if you can just make employees happy they'll work harder or better as a way of reciprocating. They will of course never, ever, perform beyond the level of their competencies. **But don't let reality get in the way of psychologizing.** Recognize that if you buy into today's psychobabble, you'll be on track to fail as an executive.

Here's a bit of folklore on the subject:

> *Psychology is the industry that has turned all the old-fashioned sins of yesterday into the emotional problems of today.*

You don't "do" wrong. You are merely a puppet to your emotions. You cannot even *choose* to commit a serious crime. That would be clear evidence (to a psychiatrist) that you are a psychotic and ought to be treated for a mental disorder. Choice is out. Being victimized by your emotions is in.

This provides employment for legions of people, and gives urban strangers something to talk about (as in Woody Allen's movies). The assumption is that addictions (to bizarre behavior) are something over which you did not have a choice at the outset. So, more and more people simply do not comprehend the possibility that one could choose one's own destiny – or the destiny of an organization.

You want to be absolutely certain that you are one of those people who cannot even comprehend the notion of choosing – and being responsible for – your own fate.

Here's a tale that tells the tale: Bob is the boss. John is one of his underlings. It is annual performance review time as we tune in …

> Bob says, *"Well, John, it's time once again for us to review your performance over the past year. I think you did okay overall, but there are some problem areas."*
>
> John replies, *"Well, I'm not surprised. It seems like I get shafted this way every year."*
>
> Bob says, *"Well, it isn't about that. I have no intention of 'shafting' you, as you put it. I'm not that kind of person. I like you. I simply want to help you improve."*
>
> John says, *"Improve?! What makes you think you can help me do that? I'm already doing the best I can."*
>
> Bob replies, *"Well, I think … I believe – that you should* ***want to*** *get better at what you do."*
>
> John says, *"Maybe* ***you*** *do.* ***I*** *don't. Actually, I think this is a pretty shitty place to work. I come to work. I do my job okay. I don't see what your problem is. If there's a problem, I think you're the one who has it. Not me. I don't much think about it. Are we going to be much longer? I think I'm getting a headache."*
>
> Bob says, *"Well, I don't think it really is my problem. I think it is your problem. We won't be long. Would you like some aspirin? The thing is, John, that this isn't my problem. I think it's more your problem."*

> John replies, *"I thought you called me in. I didn't ask you to help me with your problem. I'm cool."*
>
> Bob says, *"Well, I'd like to get specific. You caused an accident that cost us a lot of money last March. I don't think that's 'cool.' And you do have a sexual harassment charge hanging over your head."*
>
> John says, *"Oh, that bitch. She's had it in for me for a long time. I suppose she'll get a good review because she blew the whistle on me, when I didn't do nothin'."*
>
> Bob replies, *"And the accident with the fork lift?"*
>
> John says, *"Wasn't my fault. I was doing just what I was supposed to be doing. Somebody else stacked those boxes where they weren't supposed to be. Bob, you know ... These sessions always bring me down. I feel "de-motivated," to use a term I heard in a recent training session with the HR broad. You make me really feel bad – not about myself so much, but about this stupid place. I feel like you just don't like me."*
>
> Bob replies, *"Well, I'd like to talk about that. Maybe we can get to the bottom of this by exploring your attitude about your work."*
>
> John says, *"I'd have a better attitude if you'd stop picking on me."*

And so on, and so on. Sound familiar? This is not about performance. This is a debate about whose feelings take precedence. It's a debate that's irresolvable.

Remarkable – how "I" went from a concept that barely existed in the previous century, to the most frequently used word in the English language. **More remarkable is how people's personal feelings went from being private to being the centerpiece of most interaction between people.** But this all plays right into your hands. Your failure would be much more difficult if these conditions were not in place.

Since there is no real world in psychology-land, discussing real-world issues is out of the question. It's just your opinion vs. mine.

Here are the practical issues:

- Most executives are on an ego trip ("ego" being a Freudian concept that is only about 100 years old). This means you come to work to perform for yourself, bringing along your feelings of the day. Elevate this to an incorrigible modus operandi.
- It has become axiomatic in our culture that performing one's duty (or even one's promises to oneself) is dependent upon whether or not one "feels like" doing so.
- Encourage this in others by being the role model for them.
- Understand that it is an adolescent outlook to assume that one is on earth to have emotional wants and needs, and to expect those to be attended to NOW. Most people these days never outgrow their adolescence. Certainly you must not.
- The focus is off of performance (duty?), what you owe yourself and others, and onto your "rights" and what is owed to you. Take this position at all times.
- Psychology is about manipulating and being manipulated, not in any real world but in the "psychological" one of feelings and emotions

and victimization. Be the exemplar for others to follow. Be the victim of your "feelings."

- The psychological world is made up of explanations and excuses, never real accomplishments. Keep your eye on the ball. Any real accomplishments by you or others who work with you would be clear evidence of being off track. Have an excuse for every shortfall always ready and waiting. Be a master of psychobabble.
- Nothing will help you more than using yourself as your role model.
- As your own role model, you can look in the mirror and see everything you need to know, or feel. Self-absorption. Perfect – for your ultimate purpose.

In his 1945 diary, British writer and critic James Agate wrote,

> *"A professional is a [person] who can do his job when he doesn't feel like it. An amateur is a [person] who can't do his job even if he* ***does*** *feel like it."*

Fill your organization with amateurs (beginning with yourself) and hope for professional performance. That never works. Hopeful incompetence: the mantra for your successful failure.

Sometimes we pretend we have really grasped something that is difficult to understand merely by announcing whether or not we "liked" it. But, as Groucho Marx once said about a play he attended:

> *"I didn't like the play, but then I saw it under adverse conditions – the curtain was up."*

Second Lesson:

Measure performance by how you feel about it.

Measure performance by how you feel about it, and let feelings substitute for accomplishments. It's a great formula for failure.

If you listen carefully, what you will hear people talking about is how they feel about things. They will spout psychobabble for hours on end, but never reveal accomplishments or performance issues. This kind of talk is almost like a modern taboo – it is socially unacceptable to be talking about what you have accomplished or any specific plans for your better performance in the future. After all, people won't perceive you as a victim of circumstances unless you play that role well.

In your quest to be a magnificent failure, you must be the "victim" of circumstances that are more powerful than you are. **Cave in to your feelings of the moment. Make the process of getting from here to your destiny one that is wholly a matter of feelings.** Fit in. You can't help the way you are, the way you feel. If you don't feel like accomplishing your goals in life, today, tomorrow, or ever, your feelings should justify that. It's certainly not your fault.

Play the role of being overworked, unappreciated, and put upon by others and by sheer happenstance. Assemble a support group for this. Blackmail those you can't recruit by being always on the verge of some psychological disorder – which would be their fault.

Above all, lead with your feelings about things. Get irritated if others try to do the same. There just isn't time for everyone to complain. They'll have plenty of time to talk about their feelings when they're the boss – having learned from you, the master. Be *known* for your feelings.

That's cheaper and faster than being known for your achievements. How can you fail to fail, if others think you're always on the other path?

Recipe #18

How to Practice Dilettantism

Dilettante: ***a person who cultivates an area of interest ... without real commitment or knowledge.***

Dilettantes never really accomplish anything. They are "collectors." They collect all kinds of esoteric and useless information about how to "succeed." They remain loyal customers for the business press. Loyal because they never put the information to the test, they merely talk about it and wait until the next newest panaceas come off the press.

The business press is in the business of feeding dilettantes. They do this by sprinkling the latest fairy dust in mainstream publications – with advice for making your organization excellent that, if you are a primo dilettante, you would never use except to talk about it with other dilettantes.

A technique, or program, broadcast as a mass solution to a particular problem is a sort of one-size-fits-all tool or technique. That means it fits no one in particular. That's okay, because they know their audience is comprised mainly of dilettantes – that is, of managers and executives who want to say, "The idea of the month is out, and this is what we're going to do now," with no real commitment or understanding of what needs to be done and why.

It used to be that dilettantish managers and executives drove people crazy, changing course every 30 days or so … or whenever the boss happened to read something that was touted as being the answer to all his problems. But now the minions have caught on. ("They may be crazy, but they're not stupid," as the old saying goes.) They know when the magazine or newspaper lands on the boss's desk, and they know that there will be much chest-thumping and launching of initiatives. Somewhat like "the panacea of the month." They know that this too will pass, roughly at the time the next panacea arrives on the boss's desk. So they make no commitment, either. They just hold their breath until the next panacea gets blown up with management enthusiasm - i.e., hot air.

The lesson? Become a world-class panacea-of-the-month executive. That way you can talk a good story but never commit to anything. You'll fail because your people will be wary of following you, even to the local coffee shop.

First Lesson:

Be a great faddist.

Dilettantes are faddists. They are always on top of the latest fads. A good dilettante can point out a fad in the latest issue of Businessweek faster than a bird dog on a fall hunting trip can point out quail in the bushes. They want to outtalk their peers, knowing the latest fads in management or leadership before the others have heard of it. As the old wisdom has it:

> *"A faddist is a person who is always giving up something new, and taking up something newer."*

Dilettantes are also advice-mongers. They don't seek advice in order to follow it – otherwise they would be using better sources. They seek advice in order to tell others what's what. They pontificate in front of their staff in order to impress them.

A dilettante knows that things are status-giving not because they work in measurable ways, but simply because they are "new." Six-sigma offers you no competitive advantage whatsoever if your competitors are practicing it more beneficially than you are. But it may make you feel superior to talk a good story. If you plan to fail, talking a good game is always far better than playing a good game.

Again, here's the old wisdom:

> *"There's no fool like the fool who is always asking for advice, except the fool who is willing to oblige."*

Or this variation:

> *"Advice is an opinion given by someone who can't use it to someone who won't."*

Fine recipe for failure: Pawn off as much advice as you can on people who won't use it. After all, you didn't use it. Why should they? It'll make you feel important, while slowly but surely becoming irrelevant because you've never accomplished much of anything beyond providing others with useless advice.

So dilettantism is an avocation. It is raising the amateurism of merely dabbling in the current fads and fashions to the level of a career. Leave a trail of the past "flavors of the month." You want people to know you for the kind of trail you leave.

As the writer Israel Zangwill put it:

> *"Every dogma has its day."*

And then, like a roman candle, it fizzles and is forgotten.

Second Lesson:

Champion every fad that has talk value.

You should champion every fad having talk value that comes your way. This will enable you to look good (smokescreen) while you avoid doing any good.

Dilettantism is being dogmatic first about this, and then about that. And then about something else. To the dilettante hooked on an idea, it is THE thing. But only until a more popular or fashionable celebrity (person or idea) comes along.

Let's look at this in action. Joel enters Ted's office. Ted is the head of operations in the company they both draw paychecks from. Joel sits down and throws his feet up on Ted's desk.

> Joel: *"Well, boss, what's the news from this morning's meeting of the highly-anointed?"*
>
> Ted: *"Interesting you should ask. Get your feet off my desk. Someone might see you. The news is that the big boss wants to install an ERP system. So you've got some agonies coming up ahead."*
>
> Joel: *"We don't have to get serious about this, do we? What happened – the old man went to another fashion show of the latest ideas about how to solve all his problems in one swell foop?"*

Ted: *"Yes, we're stuck with this one. I think he's forgotten about his all-hands drive to become six-sigma by the end of the year. But they're bringing in a whole staff of IT people to put this in place. They'll be around for at least six months."*

Joel: *"And we'll be stuck with the problems that get created for a couple of years, my bet. We're always dancing to somebody else's tune. In the meantime our customers suffer and all of my people are demoralized. You people ought to put the old man on a leash. We leave a trail of new ideas that get forgotten like a garbage truck with the back open. Can't you do something about all of this wasted time and effort?"*

Ted: *"Not if I want to get promoted."*

Dilettantes with power work in that great divide between ideas and commitment. They are capable of neither one. Be certain you are capable of neither one.

Not only does every dogma have its day, but **every celebrity (person or idea) has their day.** Tomorrow your guru may be outranked or outflanked by a new guru. And you have to be ready to leap aboard his or her new and improved bandwagon.

Be the kind of dilettante who doesn't know (and doesn't care) what it might take to fully understand and to implement an idea. And the kind of dilettante who commits to an idea he doesn't thoroughly understand and couldn't successfully implement if he did. Then jump on the next bandwagon. The other one will quickly fade into history after wreaking havoc on your organization. Make sure you get the credit for the damage, not "IT."

As some perceptive social observer once said,

> *"There are well-dressed foolish ideas just as there are well-dressed fools."*

Dilettantes judge an idea by the way it is packaged and sold – because they are incapable of judging it in any other way. This will serve you well. But you have to practice dilettantism until you master it. And you have to play to the fact that people are judging your book by its cover. Sordid stories of good ideas mishandled with a seductive cover will work well.

Dilettantism is the habit of appearing to be a person who knows what he is talking about even though he usually doesn't. It's sort of like being a well-spoken jester, this huge capacity you need for waxing eloquent about something you don't understand and could certainly never bring to fruition. Practice this. Be ready to die for an idea, as long as you have given no thought as to what it would take to be implemented. It'll be easy to "sell" your lieutenants on any idea so long as they know it will never be implemented. Be dedicated to your failure by being a dedicated dilettante.

And you will remember what Will Rogers said,

> *"Everybody is ignorant,*
> *only on different subjects."*

Here's the lesson: Be ignorant on all subjects that are important, but appear to know more than anyone about those subjects. Know a little bit about irrelevant subjects, and hold forth on those at great length at every opportunity.

You can't say you've never known anyone who facilitated his failure that way. A dilettante is a person who loves to talk about the latest and greatest ideas in the arena of fashionable ideas, but who hasn't given much thought to specifically how they would be – or could be – implemented. The magic lies in being enchanted by the idea.

The latest and greatest ideas are usually elevated to the heavens by "buzz," but then dropped unceremoniously when the next one comes along. Many executives seem to be able to talk only about what they've heard. They can't talk much about what they've been thinking – because, if you remember that recipe, they can't be both thinkers and failures. So they tell people what they've heard, or read, and pretend it was their idea.

Most people are amateur or part-time dilettantes. To raise your dilettantism to the level of virtuosity will require you to exaggerate.

Watch the dilettantes you know and out-perform them. Like a roman candle, go off with explosive enthusiasm as every new idea comes along.

After your ardor cools in the heat of the next idea, begin to question people about where they got that previous nonsense.

It's a fun game – accusing your followers of being stupid for being taken in by ideas that can't work (on their own). They'll never figure out that you are the wrong message, if you develop them as dilettantes. They'll help you to fail.

So will your peers and your superiors, unless they are dilettantes, too. If they are, out-perform them as a dilettante, and you will be a source of constant irritation to them. That'll work.

Recipe #19

How to Reward B While Hoping for A

You'll again find yourself in a crowd here. Most executives and assorted managers, administrators, parents, and teachers do this routinely. They thoughtlessly reward certain behaviors even though their "hope" is to encourage different behaviors.

Those who are really good at this way of failing in their roles have been known to reward the very performance or behavior they *don't* want. For example, parents often tell their children to stop whining, doing so in a very whiny voice. Managers (and executives) will frequently reward people for *activities* while actually "hoping" for *accomplishments*.

It's just barely possible that they engage in this marginally insane way of doing things because they've tried it on themselves, found it doesn't work, so they feel comfortable in applying it broadly in their organizations and in their lives. For those who are on the path to failure, it seems that the less able they are to "motivate" themselves to do right, the more convinced they are that other people can be "motivated" to do right.

"Motivation" is perhaps the central fixture in the belief system of people who are on the path to failure. So cling to it as a drowning person clings to anything that looks like it will keep you afloat. Or such people may simply be incompetent – and the unworkable things they believe in so strongly are merely manifestations of that incompetence. If you're doing this right, you will actually come to believe that hope *IS* a method. If you use hope as a primary method, you're almost bound to fail. The more you replace actual performance with mere "hope," the more expeditiously you will fail. So – a great tool for your toolbox

First Lesson:

Make hope one of your central management tools.

Here's how you can make this work for you. If you make hope one of your central tools for managing, and if you very astutely provide recognition and reward systems that encourage behaviors you don't want, all the while "hoping" your minions will produce the performance you do want, you will have made a significant contribution to the cause of your failure. Not that difficult. It's done every day by people who don't even intend to fail. Your passion for your cause will enable you to surpass all of those half-hearted executives and managers who do this every day, but unwittingly.

There are two underlying aspects of this recognition and reward business that you should know about.

One is about the source and consequences of "incentives" in general. Concepts like "incentives" and "motivation" came from experiments with lab animals (you know, rats and pigeons) years ago. The research demonstrated that if you deprive these critters of food or sex, they will crave what they have been deprived of, and will literally jump through hoops (or run mazes faster), if the "reward" of food or sex is offered.

If that's what you think of your people, if you think they have the mentality of lab rats or of pigeons, go for it. Take the position that you already know what mental cripples they are. All that's left to do is to negotiate the price for getting them to do what you want them to do.

That's one. The other one is this: There has never yet been an "incentive" program devised that people can't beat. So what actually gets rewarded is their effort in figuring out how to beat the system you put in place. They may act like clunks at work, but when it comes to how to beat the incentive system, they'll outwit you every time.

That is how trying to reward one performance often turns out to reward a quite different performance. When you tie executive performance to stock price, as we all well know many Fortune 500 companies now do, what you get are greedy executives who spend more time reading the ticker tapes than paying attention to the basics of the business. See how you can make incentive systems work for your purposes?

Getting people to pay attention to the wrong things will ensure your failure. **If you were not hell-bent on failure, you'd want ROA – Return on Attention.** But attention to what? If you can devise systems – especially incentive systems – that draw their attention more than their work does, you will have another accelerator in your failure engine.

If you provide sales people, for example, with commissions on *sales*, you will encourage many of them to be revenue-chasers. Revenue is but one of many critical issues in running a healthy and robust company. If the sales people are chasing revenue, they will have their focus not on what's good either for the customer or their own organization. Their attention will be focused on what's good for *them*. Your failure is further assured in creating such stupid reward systems. Do it.

Parents will often bribe their children to try to get them to do what they want them to do. When the children are older but now cleverer and have become experts at the bribery/extortion game, the parents realize it didn't work the way they wanted it to. In fact, the children – just like managers and other incentive junkies – will drop their previous digs without compunction if they find better places to play the bribery/extortion game. Make your organization a "destination" for people who are looking for an easier way of making a buck than earning it!

Incentive reward systems constitute a **form of bribery** for the executive and a **form of extortion** for those who are looking for personal gain from the best game in town. What the extortionists want is more incentives for even less performance. What the incentivists want is more performance. **Experienced extortionists always win.**

Scene: a very large electronics distribution firm. The CEO admitted he didn't understand the complex incentive system devised to get better performance out of a very large cadre of salespeople (several hundred). They did. They thought their job was to win the incentive game, not orders from actual customers. With the help of the salespeople themselves, the incentive system would have put the company out of business. But the CEO trashed it, out of sheer desperation, thus saving the company. The lesson for you? If you've got something that works that well, but in the wrong direction, keep it going. Reward **B**, while pretending to be hoping for **A**.

The "game" turns out to be "How to get paid more for no more." Most employees know how to play their part. And most managers know how to play their part.

For example:

> *On the shop floor, most employees will manipulate the standard cost numbers so their "bonuses" kick in earlier.*
>
> *One CEO who got caught cooking the books couldn't understand why employees would do such a thing as manipulating the work standards "just to make a little more money."*

The lesson here seems clear enough. Be as greedy and as self-indulgent as you wish when no one is looking. When people are looking, denounce every form of greed and materialism. That way, the sins of hypocrisy will make an added contribution to your failure.

In the following brief exchange Jack, the new CEO, is talking to his consultant, Alice, about his desire to put in place an "incentive" program for his managers:

> Jack: *"So I've been reading a lot about how just the right incentive program for managers increases the company's performance across the board."*
>
> Alice: *"It happens sometimes. Do you know the book,* ***Punished by Rewards****? Generally speaking, incentives like bonuses tend to backfire. What do you want to accomplish with a bonus or incentive scheme?"*
>
> Jack: *"Well, I don't read much. Too busy. Besides, I think experience is the best teacher. What would I want to accomplish? I want my people to be more dedicated and to perform at a higher level."*
>
> Alice: *"Do you think money increases their competence? When you took on your new role,*

were you thinking that now that you had been promoted and had lots more income, you were 'motivated' to be smarter and more competent? If so, it didn't happen, did it?"

Jack: *"I work long hours in this job. I love being the boss. I don't need an incentive."*

Alice: *"So what would it take, money-wise, to make you into the best CEO who ever lived? Did you overnight become a better CEO because you got the promotion and the additional financial considerations?"*

Jack: *"Well … no. But it helps."*

Alice: *"How **would** you 'incentivize' yourself to be a better CEO than you are? If you don't think you need it, what makes you think that other people will perform at a higher level if they are 'incentivized'?"*

Do incentives work? Or, at the end of the day is this just a way of playing the bribery/extortion game, a game that both ultimately lose? Lesson? Play the game. It will aid you in your cause to fail.

Second Lesson:

Play the incentives extortion/bribery game.

Incentive systems generate fascination, but they don't generate any competence. Have you noticed that there is almost never any reward for finding fault with shortfalls of competence? There's an old saying:

There's often a reward for finding something, but never for finding fault.

Never commend yourself for discovering your own faults or shortcomings. Be the kind of person who routinely rewards yourself for "doing your best." That way you will never know what your best might actually have been. So you can then openly reward others for merely doing their jobs "as best they can." Mislead them as you have misled yourself.

Good example: In the typical organization, the "squeaky wheel" usually gets the "grease." Executives spend more time with and about poor performers than they do with and about high performers. To fail illustriously, adding more grease to the squeaky wheel is a useful recipe to follow.

It is a relatively benign form of insanity that will serve your cause well. Most "incentive" systems are stupid systems. Why is that?

They assume that people are about as stupid as a lab rat. They assume that the level of performance is indirectly controlled by the level of incentives. They assume that executives and the people who do the work of the organization are two different species. They assume that incentives directly impact competence. They assume that if you (actually) reward the wrong behavior, but hope that this will get people to the right behavior, it just might happen. It won't.

Rewarding **A** does not get you to **B** no matter how much you hope it will.

And therein lies your advantage. Devise stupid reward systems and they will ensure your failure. You just have to be certain that people put the blame on you, and not on the system. But, heck, that's the way it works now, isn't it? You'll know you've won when they keep the stupid system, but eliminate you.

Recipe #20

How to Play the "Explanation Game"

IF I tell you something I know but don't fully comprehend, and which may be irrelevant to what either of us needs to know (if we knew what that was) …

And **IF** you tell me something you know without any real thought about whether or not it is relevant to what I need to know (if I knew what that was) …

And **IF** we repeat what we've told each other to several other people …

THEN we have created what is called a "network" or an "informal organization." Forget the organization chart. In organizations like yours, this is the "real" organization. What's said there becomes gospel for the functioning of the organization.

Organizations are networks of people who tell each other what they know. It's mainly what *they've* been told or read somewhere. They may pretend to be telling other people what those other people need to know. But, at best, they can only tell those other people what they know. The higher your level in the organization, the more your telling gets misunderstood but retold. The retelling involves the unique spin put on what you said by those who heard it. Then *they* will put another spin on it because of who they're talking to and, as it is in the "telephone game," what comes out after a retelling or two bears little resemblance to the original telling, which had *your* spin on it in the first place. **Ah, what webs of understanding and misunderstanding we "spin."**

The "lower" people are in an organization, the less attention they pay to what those in the higher echelons are saying. That's because the lower-level people know that executives rarely listen to themselves, and they almost never listen to lower-level people. These lofty people rarely visit the people who actually do the work of the organization, and are disinclined to listen to people who are (by status, at least) so inferior to them.

Explanations of why we need to do this or that in order to compete or to survive, fall on indifferent, case-hardened ears. Besides, the organization the worker-bees inhabit is never the organization as it is perceived by the lofty ones.

First Lesson:

Mine the explanation game mother lode.

Thus we are catapulted into the explanation game, the most popular and universal of all the games played in organizations. There are infinite variations on the "Why did *that* happen?" game. Those all require explanations. Here's the mother lode. Mine it and become the best player around, and you will be making a substantial contribution to your cause, which – lest you should have a momentary lapse and inadvertently court success – is to fail on purpose. And, thus, proudly.

This is how the explanation game works: Somebody in a position to tell other people what to do says, "This is what we're going to do." If challenged, he can always offer an explanation of why it has to be done. Having learnt their role well since childhood, the people who are supposed to do it now have to come back with an explanation of why it couldn't be done and/or why it didn't happen.

If challenged, they have to explain *how* it didn't happen. They know from experience that the superior who issued the order will "understand." They know this because they assume her role is to understand explanations, since she spends so much of her day fielding "explanations." They also know she will "understand" because she always seems to have an explanation ready to explain to *her* superiors (or herself) why something she had agreed to accomplish didn't get accomplished.

Find bosses who are an easy mark for explanations, so you can practice your skills. But, *as* the boss, be an even easier mark. **People will like you because it is so easy to explain to you why what was supposed to happen didn't happen.** So other subordinates who would rather explain than *accomplish* will gather around you. You can see how this will further your cause.

Another key element of the "explanation game" that you will want to ponder and use to your advantage is as follows:

All explanations are not equal. Some work better than others. Nor are they interchangeable. What works in one case with a boss won't necessarily work with a different boss or in a different situation. That's what makes the game game-y.

Winston Churchill was once asked the question,

> *"What are the desirable qualifications for any young man who wishes to become a politician?*

Churchill replied,

> *"It is the ability to foretell what is going to happen tomorrow, next week, next month, and next year. And to have the ability afterwards to explain why it didn't happen."*

He could have been talking about executives, couldn't he? Or maybe all of us. This is but an "explanation" of the kind of abilities you must hone.

We might well have been talking about "excuses" back there. But excuses are often thinly-veiled attempts to avoid blame, too easy to see through. So people become more creative.

Sometimes an excuse a parent or a boss has never heard before will gain you some brownie points for sheer imagination or just for the laughs. You should certainly **reward the creativity put into excuses** for why something that was supposed to get done didn't get done. That way you can have lots of laughs while you fail for lack of accomplishments.

There are many folksy observations that may deserve your reflection:

> *"When it comes to excuses, the world is full of great inventors."*
>
> *"We all find excuses instead of time for the things we don't want to [**or can't**] do."*
>
> *"A lie by any other name would be just as poor an excuse."*

Here are some pointers:

1. The typical organization pays more for mere activities and excuses than it does for real accomplishments. And it pays more for creative excuses than it does for lame ones. Excuses are at best non-value-added. At worst, they generate lots and lots of sunk costs. That's why they can be so useful to you and your cause.

2. It was Henry Wadsworth Longfellow who said, "It takes less time to do a thing right than it does to explain why you did it wrong." Was it a *poet* who launched the contemporary "lean" movement? People can't be depended on to do what they know they are supposed to do. If you really are determined *not* to fix that problem, you'll write it off as something those people didn't "want to" do. Nothing you can do about that. But **you** need to do better than that. You can make sure they weren't capable of doing what had to be done in the first place.
3. Most executives don't think of the failure to accomplish what someone promised to accomplish as a "lie." But it is, isn't it? A promise broken is a "lie." The more vague you can be in making assignments, and the more indifferent you can be about whether they are carried out or not, the better and more certain your pathway to failure. Let there be no consequences for lying.

One of the major sources of generating the need for explanations is, of course, forecasting. As they unravel, these fictions are typically the cause for a highly competitive "Olympics" of excuses and explanations. Malcolm Forbes once quipped:

> *"Anyone who says businessmen deal in facts, not fiction, has never read old five-year projections."*

Or as Samuel Goldwyn, who put it,

> *"Never make forecasts, especially about the future."*

Not, anyway, unless you are ready, willing, and able to dazzle everyone with your explanations for why it didn't happen the way you said it would. Your subordinates need forever to be making forecasts and projections. That's so they can have lots of experience at making excuses – needed to keep you fast on the track to your amazing failure.

Second Lesson:

Become both an excuse magnet and an excuse monger.

In the conventionally mediocre organization (and you would want no other kind), what happens is that managers and executives become *excuse magnets*. Thus your subordinates can become *excuse mongers*. Games like the "explanation game" require that the players play their part so the other players can play their part. Each has to be complicit in the other's moves. As the French essayist Montaigne wrote,

> *"When I play with my cat, who knows but that she regards me more as a plaything than I do her?"*

To encourage explanations rather than actual accomplishment, you need to expect and appreciate the one more than the other.

How could you be an excuse magnet if you haven't trained your people to be excuse mongers? What needs explaining is failure to accomplish. Spend most of your time there. Your people will figure out what they need to do fairly quickly. Only if you always have just the right words to excuse yourself for your own shortfalls can you routinely accept others' excuses for their failures to perform.

The ultimate advantage for *your* failure, however, lies in arriving at the point where you can accept an explanation (or an excuse) as a reasonable equivalent of the actual accomplishment expected.

That is, to be mutually reality-averse. As Robert Iverson (the founder of Kiwi International Airlines) once said,

> *"There's a lot of comfort in being with similarly disturbed people."*

Surround yourself with people who are committed explainers rather than doers, and provide them with a world-class role model. Being similarly disturbed, you will find a lot of comfort there and get your ticket to failure punched early and frequently.

Here's a short, short story:

> *The CEO gave the CFO an assignment.*
>
> *Then the CEO gave the CFO another assignment.*
>
> *The CFO devoted much time to worrying about which one had the highest priority.*
>
> *So he missed the deadlines for both.*
>
> *After the CFO explained his failure, they both had a few laughs about some previous golf games they had shared.*

The moral of the story for you? You must appreciate people (beginning with yourself) not for their accomplishments, but for their ability to explain away their failures. The better you can do this, the sooner you will fail.

Recipe #21

How to Miscommunicate

Most people do – "miscommunicate," that is. That's what makes this indispensable recipe so challenging.

This "failure to communicate adequately," as you might find it defined in your dictionary, is not quite right. That's the trivial view. The more profound view is that people miscommunicate because they are *incapable* of carrying out the task any better than they do.

When it comes to communication, most people are no more than marginally competent. There are three reasons this is so:

1. If you are like most people, it's almost certain that you do not understand how utterly vital communication is to the quality and direction of the life you have and the life you will have.

2. Communication is not taught well – or even rightly – at home, in school, in church, or in any organization to which people belong or in which they pursue their livelihoods. Because it is ubiquitous, we fail to see how *consequential* it is for us individually, and collectively.

3. People assume that, because they make noises out loud, or scribbles on paper, and because other people respond in some more or less reasonable way, they have "communicated." And we further assume that all of the misunderstandings that occur just go with the territory.

Let us add something vitally important to the mix:

> *Every observation you make, everything you read, everything you hear, has to be* ***interpreted. By you.***
>
> *You have to make this interpretation with the only tool you have to do it with – your own mind.*
>
> *Your tools are yours. They are not universal tools.*
>
> *Every person has his or her own agenda. Like you, each has to put a "spin" on everything that comes their way. All according to their agendas and their abilities for making the interpretation.*
>
> *This is a source of frustration for most executives.*
>
> *Like you, they typically blame the people.*
>
> *It's not the people who are to blame. It is the executives' – and others' – inabilities with respect to communication that are to blame.*
>
> *As always, "it takes two to tango." You're not going to be any better as a "communicator" than are the others you're talking to. And they are not going to be any better listeners or readers than you are as the "communicator."*

Most people – and this may or may not include you – can't ***think****. People who are not competent thinkers will never be competent communicators – either as senders or receivers.*

The prognosis isn't good.

At least not without solving the underlying problem(s).

So you can see there are infinite possibilities everywhere for you to develop your capacity to splendidly miscommunicate.

First-rate implications for your illustrious failure are all there. Did you catch 'em? Or was there some miscommunication?

Things might proceed more efficaciously if we didn't talk to ourselves all the time – coupled with assuring ourselves that we know what we're talking about – **that our internal dialogs are, if not the absolute truth, vitally important to the continuation of life as we know it on this planet.**

Communication that affects or moves people requires of the message-sender *and* of the message-receiver a whole bundle of skills – as difficult to develop and practice as those required by the world-class golfer or pianist. **To avoid casual miscommunication, you must be a masterful listener, a masterful speaker, and a masterful thinker.** Without these qualifications on both sides, communication is no more than muddling-through. Muddling-through, as every executive knows, creates more problems than it solves. But it is the muddling-through that has to get *paid for* in most organizations.

Oscar Wilde put it better than I could:

"I often have long conversations with myself, and I am so clever that sometimes I don't understand a single word I am saying."

If, like Wilde, you sometimes don't understand what you are saying to yourself, there is some danger that this will lead you to some kind of "success." But if you always understand every word of what you say to yourself, and agree with it wholeheartedly, then you have the seeds for your failure well planted and fertilized. A useful recipe for your collection.

We can make something quite useful for your purpose out of a comment provided by Milton Mayer:

> *"I have never been able to understand why it is that just because I am unintelligible nobody understands me."*

There's more here than a potential chuckle. For your purpose, this opens up all sorts of possibilities.

First, people don't want to be challenged to think about what you say. The easier you are to understand, the more they will want to have you around. So you want to make certain that your subordinates easily and readily understand everything you say. That will mean that you're all on the "same wave-length." This will contribute to your failure by making it seem that what you are talking about and what they are understanding is important for that reason alone.

But this is a two-headed paradox. You also want to make certain that your peers and your superiors *don't* understand you. The more difficulty they have trying to understand you, the more they will *not* want to have you around. And they are the people who can do something about your failure. So you need to surround yourself with like-minded people and at the same time be at odds communicatively with those who are in a position to get rid of you.

First Lesson:

Be easy to "understand," but focus on irrelevant stories and details.

If you see the failure potential in this, I advise you to get hung up on the *details* of what is being referred to. Not on what the objectives might be. Pay no heed to the consequences of your – or others' – blather. If you're having a meeting to decide what needs to be done, quibble with the facts, the stories, and the details people bring to bear. Make sure that what you say or interpret engages all the irrelevant details. In most meetings, this will happen without any conscious effort on your part. But appear to be the source of all of the irrelevancies and going-nowhere sidebars you can.

People don't want to hear the truth. They want to hear a well-crafted and plausible story. **Be the king of irrelevant story-telling and you're on your way.** And you can gain complicity from others along the way by your manner of speaking.

Do what you have to do in thus obfuscating the point so that the discussion does not slip off onto what might turn out to be a productive course.

If engendering animosity doesn't work, try apathy. As advertising executive William Bernbach said,

> *"In communication, familiarity breeds apathy."*

Good advice. This simply means that the more quantity and the less quality in your communication, the more apathetic people become. They won't care whether you stay or go. If people know what you are going to say, why do they need you around?

As Stephen Potter put it in his book, *Lifemanship*,

> *"If you have nothing to say, or, rather, something extremely stupid and obvious, say it, but in a 'plonking' tone of voice–i.e., roundly, but hollowly and dogmatically."*

Here are three commandments for miscommunication:

- Do not say what you mean. The less sure you are of what you mean before you speak or sit down to write that email, the better you will get at this.

> [We could hardly avoid the exchange between Alice, the March Hare and the Mad Hatter in *Alice in Wonderland* at this juncture]:
>
> *"Then you should say what you mean," the March Hare went on.*
>
> *"I do," Alice hastily replied, "at least – at least I mean what I say – that's the same thing, you know."*
>
> *"Not the same thing a bit!" said the Hatter. "Why you might just as well say that 'I see what I eat' is the same thing as 'I eat what I see!'"*

- Do not mean what you say. No matter what you say or read, or what you say to others, make sure it has no real consequences for them – or for you.
- Do not have clear objectives in mind. As long as you're not clear about your objectives, others can't be either – and thus miscommunication will ensue.

To paraphrase Somerset Maugham,

> *Plunge into a sea of platitudes, and with the powerful breast stroke of a channel swimmer, make your way confidently towards the white cliffs of the obvious.*

You can fail by default, or on purpose. Take the high road.

Have a very limited vocabulary, replete with clichés. Repeat them over and over again. Prefer people who can't think about what they say or what you're saying. Give clear and purposeful communication your lowest priority. One more recipe to add to your manual for success at failing.

Recipe #22

How to Prepare for What's Already Happened

One of the best predictors of exceptional potential for failure can be observed whenever the chief executive gets dozens of people involved in extensive analysis of why something unexpected happened. And then, getting them further involved in making elaborate plans for … *avoiding what has already happened.*

All this folderol would be common sense if history repeated itself. But most happenings that surprise us are "one-off." That is, they happen only once. The next happening occurs at a different time, in a different context, and with people who themselves have changed as a result of the earlier happening. (Or should have.)

As French poet and critical thinker Paul Valery put it,

> *"History is the science of what never happens twice."*

Maybe it is simply that too many executives believe they can control the future as well as the present (which, of course, they cannot). This excessive

First Lesson:

Study the unexpected and plan as if it will be repeated.

arrogance and self-aggrandizement lures them down the garden path to failure.

The more certain *you* are that you can not only predict but control the future, the more certain it is that you will achieve failure.

Above all, make a great show of "closing the barn door after the horses have escaped." That is, of investing much time and money in figuring out why the barn door was open in that specific instance. And of creating an elaborate plan for preventing it from happening in the future. It won't anyway. **But your bravado will make it appear that what you planned is why it didn't happen again.** And while so much attention is being devoted to finding a cure for what just happened, you can be blindsided by the next unexpected happening.

Getting lots of people involved helps. That way they can collectively concoct a story that purports to explain what happened. Napoleon's view was more cynical:

> *"What is history but a fable agreed upon?"*

But all this may go against your ingrained belief – so universally held – that explaining the past provides the keys to understanding the future. Not so. Consider this:

> *Even knowing everything there is to know about how something (usually bad) happened in the past does **not** provide anyone with the qualifications or the competencies for making something (good) happen in the future.*
>
> *It is therefore far better to invest your time and energies in accomplishing future goals than in analyzing past shortfalls.*
>
> *Besides, why would you want to "learn" – perversely in **this** way – how to do something wrong?*

Prediction is fraught with error and delusion - about people and their behavior, and especially about the unpredictable outcomes when two or more people engage in competition or in collaboration. In either case, there is not much that can be envisioned with any certainty. Here's how James T. Adams reckoned the difficulty of such prediction:

> *"Any astronomer can predict just where every star will be at half-past eleven tonight; he can make no such prediction about his young daughter."*

Here are the immediate lessons for those who have failure as their cause:

- Spend as much time as you can and involve as many people as possible in what usually amount to witch-hunts.
- The opportunities are limitless. That's because the actual cause is most likely to be someone's (or some group's) incompetence. But that will not be openly considered, nor become a part of the conclusions. Thus the actual cause will continue to bear on the future.
- When was the last time you heard someone (or yourself) say, "No need to look further for a scapegoat (like 'the economy' or those dolts over in shipping), because the problem was actually caused by *my* incompetence"? Finding a "cause" unrelated to people's competencies for dealing with the unexpected ensures that stupid problems will occur again … and again.

If you are careful never to fix this basic cause of most problems, you can mount witch hunts forever. That's because, for most people, incompetence is presumed to be ineradicable – especially so if it is their own.

Short, and merciful, a story: Will is the CEO of the company he founded. He is in session with his operations manager. We'll call him Chuck.

> Will says, *"Dammit, Chuck. Somebody screwed up and my best customer is mad as hell. I want you to get to the bottom of this – you know, find out exactly why this shipment got screwed up."*
>
> Chuck says, *"Well, Will … It got screwed up mainly because what you said they wanted and what they said they wanted didn't jibe. And it was a rush project, as you know."*
>
> Will says, *"Damn right it was a rush project. We'll always bend over backwards for our best and oldest customers."*
>
> Chuck replies, *"When we do that some other customer gets the short end of the stick – you know, limited resources and all."*
>
> *Chuck made his "report" to Will some days later. In it, he concluded that the problem was caused by a supplier, and there was a difference of opinion about whether the supplier had shipped what they were supposed to ship.*
>
> *So a new procedure was established, on top of all of the new procedures that had previously been established to solve a problem that had already occurred. The procedures were often contradictory and confusing. But they grew and grew. And they began to have more problems with the procedures than they used to have with the processes.*

Always solve a problem by establishing a new procedure. This will make it look like you're doing something positive when you've actually compounded a non-problem by *preparing* for what's already happened.

The widely-known "philosopher" Soren Kierkegaard put it in these terms:

> *"Life can only be understood backwards.*
> *But it must be lived forwards."*

The lesson for those who want to fail is fairly obvious: Always back into the future by looking where you've been. Prepare only for the expected. Focus only on understanding past problems. The future is something that is *made*. If you do not do what needs doing to make it for your purposes, the world will make it for you. Don't let those arbitrary forces be inadvertently successful. Choose the right horse to ride.

The lesson for managers who will fail in spite of their hope otherwise is to do what Churchill suggested:

> *"I always avoid prophesying beforehand*
> *because it is much better to prophesy after*
> *the event has already taken place."*

Still, you have to be clever about this, in order to out-do the hordes of others who are doing the same thing. Get paid for making elaborate analyses of past events, and elaborate plans for avoiding what has already happened. Be oblivious to the implications of the following observation by one of our most useful provocateurs, George Bernard Shaw, who wrote,

> *"We learn from history that we learn*
> *nothing from history."*

To pursue your cause, assume that everything you need to know can be learned from analyzing the past, that is, from experience, which is *your* history. Prepare yourself for what has already happened.

This is perverse logic – looking at the past to decide how you should do things in the future. You can't prevent a problem with the same set of minds that created it in the first place. Successful leaders create the problems they want – or need. People who fail pit themselves against fate or happenstance with the same incompetencies that gave rise to the problem in the first place. Remember that formula and practice it until it becomes second-nature to you.

Randomness is a powerful adversary. **You will never defeat randomness.** But, to fail expeditiously, you must spend a lot of time and effort attempting to do so.

Try to control what you can't control, and fail to control what you can.

Make a plan that is independent of people's competencies. Don't identify incompetence as the culprit. Could lead you to success. Put all of your eggs in the basket (the plan) with which *you intend to defeat the world's randomness*. If you have a recipe that always seems to turn out badly, cling to it with all your might.

Recipe #23

How to Own Other People's Problems ... So They *Can't*

Here's what that means: If you own someone else's problem, they can't own it. That's the nature of ownership. You take over a problem that ought to belong to someone else, and now you own it and the other person can't because you do.

This works for the problems and the processes in your organization as much as it does for the house you live in. The problems the previous owners had with it are now yours. Most people would prefer not to own their own problems – especially if owning them would require a lot of time or effort. It's like pick-pocketing in reverse. They slip something to you that they don't want, without your realizing it at the time.

Or you may *want* others' problems, just to show how superior you are. By assuming they are stupid, you intervene. And then you own what they don't want to own. Way to go, way to fail.

Getting just the right problem owned by just the right person at just the right time is the underlying dynamic of any extraordinary organization. How you fail, and how your organization fails, is by having the wrong problem(s) owned by the wrong person(s) at the wrong time. This may seem like a difficult thing to do. It isn't. It's done every day in every way in almost every organization. If you own your subordinates' problems, or if it is assumed the organization owns their problems, they can't own them. Or at least they don't have to.

The best example is performance. Managers often think that the performance of the people who work under them is a management problem. Subordinates are quick to learn that this is okay by them. They come to work, do more or less what they're told, and the resultant problems belong to the boss. It's insane, of course. But this is the way you've got to play the game if you want to fail. And if you want to fail illustriously, make sure that most of your time is spent dealing with the problems that arise because you've got the wrong person owning the wrong problem.

First Lesson:

Spend your time on "wrong person/wrong problem" problems.

It's an old story, still useful:

There was this high-level executive who had a son. He tried all the tricks he knew to get the son to tend his yard with conscientiousness, with real competence and attention to detail. He tried bribery. He tried all sorts of incentives. He even tried hollering, and the standard threats.

But it never happened.

What did happen was that the son grew up, got married, and had a lawn of his own. The son's lawn was the best in town – beautiful, lush, perfectly groomed.

The father, executive that he was, wondered and wondered what had made the difference.

Most executives prefer a problem they can't solve to a solution they don't like. So this father may still be wondering.

The solutions we don't like are typically those that would require us to change our beliefs, to get out of our well-worn mental ruts.

Let's consider a universal example:

A person comes to work at your place. Doesn't belong there. Shouldn't have been hired, but you know how those things go.

This person's main aim was to get a regular paycheck. Beyond that, he didn't much care.

Comes time for that infamous "performance appraisal." The assumption is that you have to tell him how's he's been doing. You function somewhat like a policeman, who has to explain to the driver what he's done wrong, as if he didn't know.

In this world, we don't want people to own the problem of evaluating their own performance. That would take away the manager's primary reason for existence –"managing" one's subordinates – like you're their mother.

You're inclined to tell this person he isn't performing up to the level desired by you.

Since his job description is made up primarily of activities, he argues that he has "done his job" – he has carried out those activities. In fact, as he argues, he is doing "the best he can."

You think there should be evidence of some accomplishments, but those are for you to know and him to find out – if he has any interest in such "management" responsibilities.

He disagrees with your judgment. So, after an hour or so, you say that, under the circumstances, you can only recommend the average increase in pay. Cowardly, but you have more of these encounters scheduled today. He says, "Okay," leaves, and you have another period of time up ahead to put up with his shortfalls.

You wonder why he looks at it that way. He wonders why you look at it that way.

And the beat goes on.

"Performance Appraisal," that's where the rubber hits the road. By this point in your life, you've been both the appraisee and the appraiser. If it seems that they don't really make sense from either point of view, it's because the wrong person owns the problem. This is a wonderful wide-open opportunity to fuel your own failure.

Own the problem of the subordinate's performance, and try to fix it. You won't be successful. But that's just the point. **In fact, make sure that the wrong person always owns the problem. Or simply that it's the wrong problem.** The outcome will always be negative. And then all you have to do is make sure that you own the outcome. An almost perfect recipe for failure.

The more competent people are, the tougher they are on themselves. They don't need someone standing over them with a stick or a carrot. The less competent people are – which of course includes most people – the more certain they are that the problem of their competence and/or their performance is not their problem. In other words, competent people *own* all of the problems related to their own competencies and their own performance. Marginally competent people expect *someone else* to own their problems: managers, the organization, society, the government, their mother, etc.

So, in order to arrive at the end-game (**failure**) by choice and ahead of most of your peers who arrive there by default, you must follow these instructions:

- You must own the problems of your subordinates' competencies, and of their performance. If you do this well, they will also expect you to own the problems of their financial security, their health, their happiness, and in general the quality of their lives at work – if not beyond.
- At the same time, you must *not* own the problems of *your own* competencies or your own performance. You must leave these problems to be owned by your superiors so they can fulfill their own moves toward the end-game.
- Keep in mind that, if yours is a mediocre organization, this will simply be "Standard Operating Procedure." You have to do it in such a forethoughtful and comprehensive way that you stand out from all the others.

As has long been known – *it is only the mediocre who are always at their best.* That's why they are so arrogantly self-satisfied. Be that way, relentlessly, on your way to glorious failure.

More considerations: To *own* a problem means that you also own the problem of seeing the problem. As G. K. Chesterton once wrote,

> *"It isn't that they* [these "mediocre" people] *can't see the solution. It is that they can't see the problem."*

To *own* a problem means that you own the problem of seeing it and defining it in the first place. People who make something of their lives understand this. Those who don't, don't.

And it also means that you own the problem of solving the problem. Robert Hutchins made this relevant observation:

> *"To solve a problem it is necessary to think. It is necessary to think even to decide what facts to collect."*

And this in turn means that if you and your people are a little to a lot short of this ability to *think,* then your movement toward your end-game has been facilitated.

To *own* a problem means that you also own the consequences of what you do or do not do about it. Parents and managers seem predisposed to shield their dependents from the real-world consequences of their choices and judgments.

Choices and decisions have consequences. **To be protected from the consequences of choices means that the ability to see and to solve problems is eroded until it ceases to exist.** That's why so many people are convinced that their problems are not their problems. They feel helpless to do anything about them, which, indeed, they now are.

Here's your lesson:

Identify your subordinates' problems for them. Solve their problems for them. And buffer them against the consequences. That way, they will fail. And by cleverly owning their problems for them, your own failure will be facilitated.

Two tips:

- Being in the role you're in, near the top of the heap, you will be well aware of the fact that your problems came from the solutions of the previous generation of executives. And the solutions you implement will become the problems of the succeeding generation of executives. So if you do a really bad job of this – making sure that your solutions will create even more onerous problems for those who come after you, you will gain a legendary reputation as a failure.
- As American humorist, Evan Esar, put it,

  > *"The world is full of problem children, and most of them are over twenty-one years of age."*

This is surely a piece of cake. Just make certain that these problem children remain dependent on you by owning *their* problems … so they don't have to. Or can't. Since it will look like you are doing what you are supposed to be doing, they will fail and take you with them. But don't go down quietly. Complain all the way that they didn't do what you told them to do. That way you can get part of the credit for their failure, as well as your own.

Recipe #24

How to Pick the Wrong Facts

A turn-of-the-century clergyman by the name of Samuel Crothers said,

> *"The trouble with facts is that there are so many of them."*

Indeed.

It has been fashionable in recent decades to lament the increasing deluge of information. As in "information overload." But the problem is not the amount. It is the relevance of the information available.

Here's the bottom line: People who have a very clear idea of what they are trying to accomplish do not have much difficulty separating the wheat from the chaff – the useful information from the irrelevant. People who are just sort of drifting along with the tides of the times are indeed confused, overloaded, and victimized by the information tsunami.

The mediocre people are going to fail by default. Since you have a specific aim in life – to fail with equanimity – you won't have much trouble sorting out what you need from what is irrelevant to your cause. The more diffuse your focus, the more likelihood there is that you could expose yourself to the wrong kinds of facts and end up going the opposite direction. You could, of course, be indifferent, and just collect whatever information happens to come your way. But then you would not be a notable failure – only an embarrassingly mediocre one.

But let's go back to square one. The favorite philosopher of the successful is Nietzsche. Not that they always understand him. They don't have to. Successful people are not into "understanding." They are into action, accomplishment. No analysis paralysis for them. What Friedrich said was,

"There are no facts, only interpretations."

What this means is that the search for the facts is a red herring. To observe a "fact" requires observing it through the lens of a human interpretation. *"Facts,"* as we all know, "*do not speak*" (as the famous physicist/ mathematician, Henri Poincare, warned).

So talking about a fact requires mutual interpretation. The fact is whatever it is. To talk about it means we interpret it – translate it into something we can talk about to ourselves and to each other.

Potential lessons abound:

- The first one is that a fact might help you get where you are going only if you have a specific destination in mind. As Alice was rudely reminded in *Alice in Wonderland*, if you don't care where you're going, there's no way to determine what facts you need to get there.

- The second one is that the poorer you are at interpreting facts, the more likely it is that you will collect the wrong facts.
- The third one is that just because two or more people are arguing about "the facts" doesn't mean they are talking about something that is independent of their interpretations. They are, "in fact," arguing mainly about their differing interpretations.
- A fourth one: If you hang out with people who think like you do, you will agree on the facts. This doesn't mean you have mutually grasped any reality. It merely means you agree with each other's interpretations. The escalation of mutual lust must work something like that.
- How two or more people *talk about* the facts will have consequences. It isn't the facts themselves that have consequences. It is how you or I or "we" interpret them. So it makes a difference how a person talks about facts, and with whom.

Pretending to have no particular aim in life will be helpful. This makes it easy to surround yourself with people who have no particular aim in life. You'll have a pretty easy time of it, failing together. And always take the position that *your* interpretations are infallible. That, like Sergeant Joe Friday, you deal only with the facts and nothing but the facts. Maybe one more suggestion: Always assume that no further facts could possibly change your mind.

First Lesson:

Assume your interpretations of "the facts" are infallible.

Einstein insisted that …

Facts are never independent of the mind of the person who perceives them.

Also keep in mind that you will get addicted to certain kinds of facts. **This addiction will make you blind to other facts.** It is what they mean to *you* that determine which facts you collect or consider. Thus they are highly selected. That's because they get their meaning or importance from *you*. Facts have no intrinsic meaning or value.

The way you think is like a butterfly net. You will catch in it whatever your mind is capable of catching. If it's garbage in, it will be garbage out.

In order to keep your failure on the fast track, you need to take the position that all facts have intrinsic meaning or relevance – incontrovertibly the meaning or relevance YOU give to them.

A short, short story:

Cliff, the guy who owns and runs the place, has asked his long-time secretary to do a little sleuthing to tell him what his people ***really*** *think of him. You know, "The facts."*

She tells him she already knows. He says, "No, I want you to get 'the facts.'"

Some days later, she reports back. "They generally think you are a horse's patoot," she says, "to put the best face on it – pun intended."

"Impossible!" Cliff retorts.

"Are you challenging the facts? Or just the fact that you don't like the facts?"

People don't give much credence to facts that contradict their beliefs.

Here's another short, short story:

> *The big boss and the sales executive are talking about customer reaction to a recent product that fails in application. The big boss says, "Can't be. The stupid customer must be doing something wrong that makes our product fail. I want you to find out what they're doing wrong and put a stop to it."*
>
> *The sales manager replies, "It could be something we're doing wrong. Besides, our deliveries are always late."*
>
> *"That's because you sales people don't know what the hell you're talking about. And we're not the culprit here. This product was my project, and it's perfect. I designed this, I know what I'm talking about!"*

The customer is always right, except when there's a challenge to some top executive's prior convictions (or, as in the little story above, his ego).

You will notice there's a bit of tension involved when one person's facts (or opinions) run afoul of another's. It isn't that the one who's paying the bill is always right. It is that there's a reality that's independent of both. No one has the market on the truth. The 'truth' is so only if YOU believe it to be so.

As has long been known,

> *Happenings do not come to us with their meanings inscribed on their backs.*

What a thing means has to be supplied by the human(s) making the interpretation. The lesson for you? Always assume boisterously and unequivocally that the way you see the world is the way the world is. And that the people who don't think so are simply wrong.

It's remarkable how the more power executives acquire, the more confidence they have that they are absolutely right. On the other hand, you *could* inadvertently be "right." This calls for some circumspection. You don't want to succeed by default.

There was a very provocative observation made by an 18th-century French soldier, Luc de Clapiers. He wrote,

> *"Reporting facts is the refuge of those who have no imagination."*

This may suggest that if you're trying to accomplish something that doesn't already exist and therefore has to be created (your *unique* failure?), imagination may be more important than facts. A unique deficit here may be to your advantage. Or disadvantage.

Surround yourself with people who assume that the answers are provided by the "facts." If you can't use the facts for your purposes they will use you for theirs.

You may recall Carl Becker's caveat:

> *"One of the first duties of [people] is not to be duped."*

Being dupe-able by what you take to be "the facts" may not be as quick as other forms of career suicide. But it is more certain.

We label as "facts" those things we just can't help believing. Or sometimes we invoke the metaphor to refer to an obstacle in our way.

We invoke "the facts" to win a point when there's a difference of opinion. We don't say, "It's only my opinion, but ..." When someone says, "It's only my opinion" – as on the internet, IMHO – it is intended to be ironic. Meaning, my opinion happens to be the truth, and yours (I say smilingly) doesn't amount to much. This kind of irony on your part will contribute mightily to your mission.

We say, "Well, the facts *are*…" when we want to one-up others in a discussion. Then we bring up certain "facts" that we have selected, put our interpretation on them, and roll them out as the definitive discussion-stopper. You know how this is done.

Second Lesson:

Master ending/winning discussions with "the facts."

Become masterful at doing it with all kinds of folk in all kinds of circumstances. That'll contribute greatly to getting you to your aim in life.

Office politics reveal that the person who gets there with facts that outweigh others' facts will win. We parry with facts. Sometimes facts are like clay pigeons, put up so others can shoot 'em down. The meeting table is often covered with blasted or ignored facts that just didn't make it.

The more power a person has, the more his or her opinions can be pawned off as facts. Be a fact-monger. Figure out what facts are going to get shot down, and champion those. It can be exhilarating to fail on purpose. Many executives succeed in spite of themselves. You have to be better than that to fail on purpose.

Recipe #25

How to Fail the Way Virgins Fail

It will come as no news to you that (sooner or later) most virgins fail in that role. That whole process could easily bring to mind the way of most young managers.

Youthful managers are like virgins. They have their eye on the position they want to have next. Their failure in their present role propels them into a higher-level role for which they are typically ill-prepared. This sets them up for failure in this new, lusted-after role.

So they strive to get in the middle of the pack and perform in a middling fashion in their new role, thinking they must have been qualified or they wouldn't be here. They may have been technically qualified for the role they *were* in. But since they got that role with little or no effort on their part, they want to rid themselves of it and move on up in the world – like virgins.

In our world, you don't get much credit for extraordinary performance in the role you're in. So you yearn to go where you get more credit. That usually requires some ambition and the lure of getting some elevated status. Not because you are qualified, but because you're supposed to *want* to "get ahead." In our culture, there is a negative connotation to being an "old maid," just as there is a negative connotation to be "just a manager." We're supposed to be "movin' on up."

Shucking one's virginity is a little like a graduation ceremony. You graduate into a status that is widely believed to be superior to the one you were in. **But you arrive there essentially unqualified for what comes next**, like motherhood or dealing with another adolescent in adult clothing who didn't deliver on his promises.

If this reminds you of "The Peter Principle," it should. The Peter Principle holds that managers and executives and the like are promoted into higher roles for which they are less and less qualified, until they arrive in a role for which they are totally incompetent.

Children want to be teenagers. Teenagers are hot to be adults. Adults want to get the stuff that comes with seniority. After a while, every one gets old and dies. Few are actually qualified and prepared to take on *that* role. As is implied by the "Peter Principle," most are going to fail – or perform no better than mediocre – in those next roles which they yearn to attain.

Virginity, like managing, is not so much a condition as it is a social role. Some play that role better than others. As Groucho Marx once quipped,

> *"I've been around so long I knew Doris Day before she became a virgin."*

We know what he meant. But no one who has been an executive wants to go back to being a junior flunky – a managerial virgin.

First Lesson:

Focus on the next role, not performing in your present one.

So, **first lesson**: Keep your eye on the prize. That's the next higher position in the hierarchy. Don't really invest too much time or effort in your present role. It's the next one where you are really going to shine. Promise this to yourself and your superiors. If they buy it, they become complicit in your failure. Then you can do the same favor for your subordinates. More money, more perks, more prestige, but only if they climb up to the next rung in the ladder. That's failing, and helping others to fail, the way virgins fail: by being dissatisfied with your present role. And by imagining that your destined role in life is the next rung up. Desire may or may not produce satisfaction. But by itself, it never produces **competence** in that next role.

Like virgins, it is the seductiveness of that next rung on the career ladder that bring so many to failure. They were never fully prepared for that next role for which they lusted.

Be ambitious to move on, assuming that – like other forms of lust – you don't need to be prepared for what comes next. Failed virgins get spouses and children. Incompetent managers get a bunch of perverse and inadequate subordinates, and both may seem stunned by the challenging realities that come with their new role.

As Madonna put it,

> *"Losing my virginity was a career move."*

And so it is for most people. To get further up on your "career" path, you have to shuck off the old role and get by hook or crook into the role that comes next.

Second lesson: If you're the boss, let your minions have no doubt, by what you say and what you do that, where they are concerned, you are in the cat-bird seat. Come and go as you please, but expect them either to be there, or to get permission not to be. Take your vacations whenever you want, for whatever length suits you. Let them know that you are always their superior. And that you can put them in their place at any time.

Make sure they understand that you make more money, have more power, and have more of all of the perks and prerogatives they want to have. Be arrogant. Make your role seem so attractive that it is seductive to all of the wannabes. This, coupled with their normal upwardly-mobile dysfunctions, will ensure their failure, and thus yours.

And make sure they are competing for your role, not consistently increasing their competence in the one they're in. Promote people on the basis of the enthusiasm they exhibit for the higher role, not for their competence in their present role.

Moving into a "higher" role does not by any means guarantee success in that role. Incumbency never raised anyone's competence. As reported in *Newsweek* (29 December 1980), Jimmy Carter's mother Lillian made the following comment at the Democratic Convention of that year:

> *"When I look at all my children, I say to myself, 'Lillian, you should have stayed a virgin.'"*

This was probably meant ironically. But it holds true for many executives. When they arrive in the top role out of lust or ambition, not out of competence and preparedness for the role, they often have regrets. But by then the mortgage and other "lifestyle" expenses are too high to consider any alternative. Besides, it seems to be impossible to return to that prior stage of one's innocence. You never know what you get until you get it.

Our culture seems to reward people according to their role, and not according to their *performance in that role*. **This would be considered stupid, if it were not so universal.** But it will serve you well in your bid to fail by intent.

Third lesson:

> *If you really believe that your performance in a "higher" role will be driven by how much you covet that role,*
>
> *Or by how much you yearn to get out of your present role,*
>
> *Then you have what it takes to fail in that role.*

People who are really, really good at what they do are not looking for more prestige, money, etc. They're too busy doing what they love to do. They know that all the rest of it will come, like the wake of a ship.

Steer the ship by looking at the wake. There's a recurrent recipe for failure.

People who are in hot pursuit of more status, more money, or more perks will not have the time or the energy to be really, really good at what they do. The algorithm of failure.

In our culture, people look down on virgins and flunkies. There is a place to be got to, a fence to leap over, a rite of passage that makes you into "somebody"– into one of "us." It's a status thing. If you've got it, it may not mean that much. But if you don't, you'll do whatever needs doing to gain it.

Virgins and flunkies do the dirty work – like Cinderella. But she failed in her role in order to become a princess. A princess has a lot of problems that scullery maids don't have – beginning with the prince and his parents, and reaching out to all of the other citizens who now expect you to be perfect. She went from being mistreated by her worldly-wise sisters and her evil stepmother to being mistreated by the king and queen and all of the other courtiers. She didn't live "happily ever after." Reality doesn't work that way.

That's a fairy tale. It never happens that way in real life – or in organizations. You can't get what you want until you give up what you had. Then it's too late.

Like most executives, what you lusted after and what you got will turn out to be mildly to wildly different. But here you are, having failed like a virgin. And no way to go back.

Many, many innocents have struggled and climbed the corporate ladder only to find that it is on the wrong wall. That's the kind failure you need. But you need to get there before others do in order to claim your prize – having failed not by default, but by choosing the most potent algorithms of failure, based on the recipes in this book.

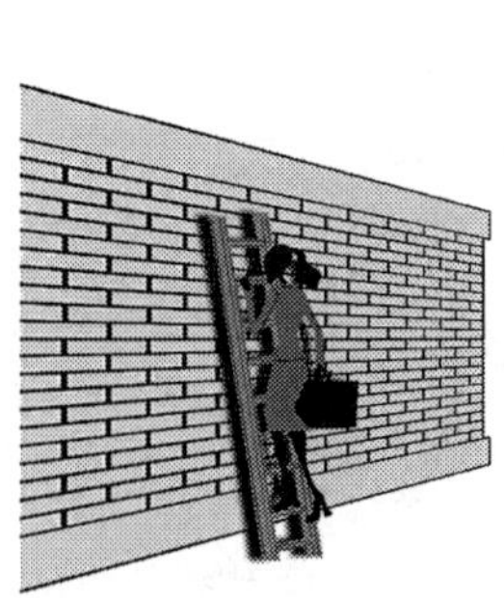

Afterword

It seemed that there was need for a place to turn things right side up again after playing around with them upside down. There are rich provocations that can be had no other way. This may be the place to do that.

There are at least three useful points to be made:

One is that ***extraordinary achievements carry more risk of failure.*** Certainly far more risk of failure than making no attempt to achieve anything beyond what one already has, or could easily achieve. Going exclusively for low-hanging fruit puts you at far less risk. One appeal of staying in one's comfort zone is in part that not much is being risked.

Thus the tyranny of the status quo: there is far more passion put into keeping yourself centered in what is familiar than of venturing into unknown territory. Most people look askance at those who take great risks, or make great efforts, or discipline themselves severely. Until one of them succeeds. Then people pretend not only that they were certain all along of that person's achievement, but they are then willing to buy fan t-shirts or other paraphernalia to identify themselves with the achiever.

Another way of looking at this is that most people would prefer vicarious exposure to the risk of failure over any actual test. Television provides a surfeit.

Here's the bottom line:

People who have no compelling goals in life risk no more than the trifling failure of conventionality and mediocrity. Those who aspire will fail. People who have never failed have never aspired to anything more than life-in-the-comfort-zone. A comfort zone is addictive. To stay out of it requires constant struggle.

A second point is that ***failure is useful to those who are determined to succeed.*** Some people fail once and give up. Even more give up without really trying. It comes down to the use you can make of failure in the cause to which you are committed. Some of our most successful entrepreneurs have early failures in their careers – e.g., Sam Walton.

More to the point, one of America's greatest inventors was Thomas Edison, whom, it was said, was a poor "businessman." He was once asked about the fact that his experiments failed more often than they succeeded. His explosive response was something like the following:

> *"I don't 'FAIL'! I simply learn how to go about something in a better way."*

Seen that way, failure can make an indispensable contribution.

A third point is that ***having nothing to lose by avoiding a cause in life is a cultural disease.*** Conventional organizations, and especially bureaucratic organizations, are typically risk-averse. What often happens is that the person who fails gets punished. This can encourage others to avoid taking any risks.

People become risk-averse. If – and when – this happens, extraordinary achievements are unlikely to occur. Avoiding risk by failing to pursue high-level achievements is one way people have of coping in such organizations.

Executives who seek to avoid failure by avoiding any commitment to achieving something extraordinary, and model this for their employees, have actually chosen mediocrity as a way of life.

Most of us, when young, had hopes and dreams for our future. But these require more discipline, more competence, or more dedication than most of us are willing to develop. So we settle. We settle for whatever comes along.

While "success" may have a mythology attached to it that the mass of people envy, "failure" has a negative connotation. So it isn't that most people actually choose a mediocre or conventional existence – getting-by. They choose instead to avoid the risk of failure.

No significant achievement can be reached from one's comfort zone. Or from the complacency that characterizes most organizations. Take the risk of failure out of life or organizations, and there goes the possibility of extraordinary achievement.

Longshoreman-turned-philosopher Eric Hoffer made this observation:

> *"There can be no freedom without*
> *the freedom to fail."*

Agreed, failing is not the same thing as achieving some worthy goal. But, recipes or algorithms for success that guarantee success – like those in the current spate of success books and magazines and conferences – do not guarantee success. They guarantee no great achievement – certainly no more than mediocre or commonplace ones. To be credible to mediocre people requires them to provide mediocre gruel.

Those who do not give themselves – or others – permission to fail in striving to achieve worthy goals are not "free." They live in a prison of their own making. **A mind or an organization (or larger culture) that takes away the "freedom" to fail takes away freedom. Period.**

Success, like failure, cannot be bought.

It has to be earned.

If your aim is to avoid the risk involved in striving toward real achievement, then the recipes in this book will serve you well. Fear of failure is a form of self-victimization. It can infect the culture of an organization or of a nation. It will make of life no more than something to be avoided by buying stuff until you become just one more item in the stuff that you've collected.

One final point: Failing in modern organizations doesn't necessarily mean you are going to get fired or removed from office. More recently, it has meant that you have the previously arranged golden parachute. This may mean that you can do better financially, without the daily struggle, if you *fail* in your executive role.

This is stupidly harmful.

If there are no real consequences for failing in your role, that may encourage any unqualified person to take it on. If you get paid as much or more for failing in your role than you would have been paid had you been successful in your role, everyone loses. Everyone loses because the logic of achievement (and even of reality) has been deformed.

It's not that people should be punished for failing. It is that rewarding failure diminishes any real interest or commitment to undertake the difficulties and work of real achievement. There are even movements underway in our schools to do away with competitiveness. There should be no winners or losers in sports. There should be no discrimination in performance or achievement. This thinking is probably all well-intentioned but again, it's also stupid and harmful.

It has been said that there are thirteen people around the world who would be willing to take on *any* job in America, and do it better. There are businesses everywhere on the globe ready, willing, and able to compete with any or all of those in America. The steel business would be an example. So would textiles. Import restrictions or other regulations are irrelevant in today's world. If we can't compete globally, we will become an also-ran. If this logic doesn't hold for executives (and teachers and parents), it will not hold for those they are attempting to lead.

If competing is passé, so is the USA.

If the only appetites executives have are the ones that drive envy and greed, then we are on the right path. If executives don't have what it takes to compete and perform in the real – competitive – world, then they will have failed not only themselves, but all the rest of us. Mediocrity has few enemies and many friends, all inmates. Real achievement propels you out of the asylum. That's a price you have to pay.

People who are in positions of power have a *moral* obligation. That is to make of themselves and their organizations all that could be made of them. That sense of moral obligation is indispensable to the *health* of any organization. Without it, there is sickness, suffering, and widespread demoralization. With it, there is a chance we could rise to our full potential – as people, as a civilization. Without it, we die.

Let me share a relevant thought from Nelson Mandela:

> *"There is no passion to be found in playing small – in settling for a life that is less than the one you are capable of living."*

If, instead, you would like to end on a smile, in keeping with the rest of the book, here is novelist Philip Roth musing on your condition:

> *"The secret to living in the rush of the world with a minimum of pain is to get as many people as possible to string along with your delusions."*

When mediocrity and incompetence trump achievement, it's a killer delusion. *Choice* is the real victim. When choosing to better yourself, to humanize yourself through the growth of your capabilities, becomes a source of ridicule, then the problem of how to live your life has been turned on its head.

Even failing on purpose has more nobility in it than failing by default.

It may be that striving to be more competent in one's role, striving to perfect oneself as a human being, is itself a delusion. If it is, we need more people to string along with it. The consequences of the alternative are too horrendous to face up to. Maybe that's why so few do so.

As Helen Keller said,

> *"Life is either a bold adventure, or it is nothing."*

It is better to fail than to live in vain.

About the Author

Lee Thayer is best known for his acerbic wit, his engaging style, his sense of humor, and for the depth and breadth of his intellectual resources. Accompany those traits with his accomplishments and the work he does in this complex world of ours, and you begin to get an idea of Thayer's vision for the "thinking, being, and doing" of leadership.

Dr. Lee Thayer, author of ***Leadership: Thinking, Being, Doing*** (2004)

Thayer's goal is to visualize the ideal, and then to figure out how to get there by starting with the actualities of the present circumstances.

Like some of the rest of us, he wants to leave this world a better place. And he's doing it – organization by organization. Many say that in his craft he has no peer. His approach is as unique (often counter-intuitive) as it is powerful. It is a life-changing experience for those who are fortunate enough to work with him.

Thayer's work begins with an invitation from an exceptional and exceptionally committed CEO – to partner with that CEO for the purpose of transforming his or her organization to an outstanding level of performance, while learning the kind of leadership required to deserve a great organization. (A high-performance organization is one that does everything it does better than anyone else – and improves upon that every day – giving that organization a *sustainable* competitive advantage.)

Thayer gets into "the trenches" with those who are going to make it happen, to help them every step of the way. As he says,

> *"It isn't what you know that creates excellence. Ninety-five percent of it is in the implementation. For that, you need a guide and a mentor – someone who's been there in all kinds of conditions."*

Dr. Thayer's career as a pioneer and influential innovator in the design and development of high-performance organizations – and in the kind of leadership required of the top executive to achieve that – has spanned more than four decades. It has often been observed that he has rattled more CEOs' cages than anyone else.

Having come from a high-level executive position in industry himself, coupled with his experience as a jazz performer and arranger and his university degrees in the humanities, engineering, and psychology, Dr. Thayer has developed a revolutionary and practical framework for understanding *what it takes* to lead the way to creating great organizations, expressively in the '*how*' as much as the '*why*'. He and his CEO partners often have to **invent** the pushes and pulls required to achieve the kind of excellence that others can't figure out how to copy.

Early on in his career, he served as consultant to several of the Fortune 500 and other notable companies, such as IBM, AT&T, Westinghouse, Boeing, Curtiss-

Wright, Pratt-Whitney, McDonnell Douglas, Phillips, Shell, General Motors, Sealtest Foods, and Hallmark. He has consulted with the U.S. Air Force, the Postal Service, numerous banks and other institutions, universities around the globe, and West Point.

He was the consultant behind the now well-known success story at Johnsonville Foods – which Tom Peters referred to as "the most remarkable example of organizational transformation" he had ever seen.

He has taken his extraordinary problem-solving skills to the Scandinavian countries (esp. Finland and Norway), to Australia, to the UK and most European countries, and to Canada, Mexico, and China. Today, he limits his work to small to medium-sized organizations where, as he says, the impact is more immediate and measurable.

His other "career," as a distinguished university professor in major universities both here and abroad (e.g., the Harvard Graduate School of Business, The University of Amsterdam, Queensland University of Technology in Australia, Universidad Complutense in Mexico, etc.) was an ongoing research project he "put up with" for thirty-five years, before "retiring" in 1991 to devote full time to his passion which, as he has described it in interviews, is

> *"... to help committed CEOs and other top executives transform themselves into leaders and their organizations into healthier, more vigorous, and more adaptive high-performance organizations."*

Doing so, many have observed, has brought life back into those organizations, and has lifted the quality of life of its employees, both at work and at home.

Dr. Thayer has been invited to work in most of the major leadership development programs in the U.S. and abroad, to share the wisdom he has gained during his many years of working and coaching "in the trenches" with his carefully-selected CEOs to make outstanding performance a way of life. Thayer has conducted hundreds of seminars and has spoken before thousands of top executives. He has served as the manager of dozens of organizations and projects, including work for the National Science Foundation, the U.S. Office of Education, and NASA.

He has been recognized as a Ford Foundation Fellow, as a Danforth Teacher, and as a Fulbright Scholar.

Truly a Renaissance man himself, Dr. Thayer is one of the most sought after seminar speakers and consultants in America.

Also by Lee Thayer,

Leadership: Thinking, Being, Doing (2004)

New Revised Edition – coming in early 2007

from *WME* Books (www.WMEBooks.com)